CROYDON LIBRARIES

This book is lent for 28 days. If it is not returned by the latest date below, a charge will be made in accordance with the Libraries' Regulations. If the book is required for a further period it should be brought back to the library for re-issue, or renewed by telephoning the number below.

GARDENS *of* Inspiration

EDITED *by*
Erica Hunningher

PHOTOGRAPHS *by*
Vivian Russell

GARDENS *of* INSPIRATION

The photographs on pages 1–5 are of Le Bâtiment, William Christie's garden in France, which is featured in Vivian Russell's chapter (pages 8–23). Along the façade of the bastide, one of four old vine trunks forms an 'aerial hedge' (page 1). The white fan-tailed pigeons that live in the pigeonnier (this page) give the garden beauty in motion (pages 2–3), as well music and song.

Gardens of Inspiration
First published in 2001
Text copyright © The Contributors 2001

Photographs copyright © Vivian Russell 2001
except for those cited in the acknowledgements on page 264

ISBN 0 563 55176 3

Published by BBC Worldwide Ltd
Woodlands
80 Wood Lane
London W12 0TT

Conceived and edited by Erica Hunningher
Commissioning editor: Vivien Bowler

Designed and typeset in Garamond by studioGossett

Printed and bound in Italy
by LEGO Spa
Colour separations by Kestrel Digital Colour,
Chelmsford

For information about this
and other BBC books,
please visit our website on
www.bbcshop.com

Contents

Preface

THIS BOOK WAS BORN of a desire to learn how celebrated gardeners look with expert eyes and where they go to recharge their batteries. I wanted to discover the personal connections that fostered their passion for plants and gardens, and to find out what inspires great garden design and plantsmanship.

Fifteen of Britain's best-loved gardeners and garden designers were invited to write about the places that inspire their life and work, choosing one garden, as well as their own, to be photographed by Vivian Russell.

A common brief, yes, but it has produced tantalizingly different interpretations. We are taken to gardens that

resonate with the art of their creators and to those eloquently described as 'otherworldly'. There are revelations of childhood and youthful influences, of 'sowing wild oats', and of places that inspired 'first love' or turned a whole world upside down. Gardens are described as 'near Nirvana' and as havens that bring 'peace beyond belief', as landscapes that shine like a 'like a beacon' on an entire gardening career. Some arouse excitement, passion, awe or even laughter. Others represent an important experience in the development of a personal design philosophy, and many have cast ripples across more aspects of a life than just gardening.

...reveals the hidden meaning of the conductor William Christie's garden in France.

Each chapter begins with a photograph of the author's own garden – some private places, others open to visitors (see pages 256–9). The garden the author has chosen to feature is illustrated at the end of the chapter, with only a few photographs within the text. Quotations from the text offer a taste of words worth savouring. It was always my intention that *Gardens of Inspiration* would be a book in which the words of eloquent garden writers are presented with the same importance as colour photographs.

The book begins with the chapter in which Vivian Russell, whose eyes and camera have interpreted the visual power of the featured gardens, reveals the hidden meaning of the conductor William Christie's garden in France. Thereafter, chapters are arranged alphabetically by author. Each is a unique journey to places that inspire the lives and work of our great gardeners.

Rhythm and Tempo

by VIVIAN RUSSELL

*The conservatory at Coombe Cottage, Borrowdale, is
battered all winter by gales and driving rain and would
look quite dreary were it not for the canopy of glossy leaves
provided by* Magnolia grandiflora. *In early spring though,
two roses, the exquisitely scented 'Climbing Columbia' and
the primrose coloured 'Safrano', are quick to flower, and*
Rhododendron fragrantissimum *is both beautiful and
intoxicating. Lilies and salvias in pots scent the conservatory
throughout the summer. Outside, my topiary pieces (seen on
page 15) were inspired by the yew bird planted forty years
ago by Mrs Hartley who lived here before me. Box and yew
revel in the wet climate (an annual rainfall of over a
hundred inches), and I have planted simple, classic shapes
that take up the theme of the fells.*

${M}$Y CAMERA HAS been my window to the world since I started taking pictures twenty years ago, but I have been looking through windows of one kind or another for as long as I can remember. My parents were great travellers. My father was in the aviation industry, and my mother liked boats, so that as a child I was forever squinting through the narrow apertures of aeroplanes, portholes and car windows as the landscapes of Europe, America, and the oceans and skies that separated them, raced by.

The excitement of travel, of trawling in new impressions and sensations has never palled. It instilled in me a great love

VIVIAN RUSSELL

The Sunday Times *described Vivian Russell's award-winning* Monet's Garden: Through the Seasons at Giverny *as 'a splendidly atmospheric photographic memoir and a perceptive and profoundly researched text'. She gardens and writes in Cumbria but travels all over the world taking photographs – of people and landscapes as well as gardens and plants. Her artistry behind the camera is matched by a gift for eloquent writing.* Edith Wharton's Italian Gardens, Monet's Water Lilies *and* Monet's Landscapes *confirmed her reputation as a brilliant writer and photographer.* ❧

of character, of the local and vernacular, and of different kinds of gardens, which I learned to differentiate and appreciate by virtue of comparison.

The first of our homes was in London where I went to Hyde Park, walking the black dachshund my parents had fallen for in the Harrods pet department. Dogs were forbidden in our apartment building and he had to be carried up and down the elevator and smuggled past the doorman several times a day, first in a small Air France bag and then, as he matured, into ever more voluminous bags which the doorman must have eyed with understandable suspicion. I loved the enormous trees in this vast public park which sparkled in spring in a dazzling array of acid greens high above me, and contrasted with the wonder of tiny things I found on the ground I could put in my pocket. Little acorns nestled in their baskets, conkers to be prized from their prickly shells, and that first flower – the daisy – and the absorbing delight of making daisy chains. I loved the damp musty smell of autumn, of burning leaves and the sound of the rooks screeching through the fog, but most of all I loved the Peter Pan statue in Kensington Gardens. It loomed above me as something absolutely magical, irresistibly tactile, the soft bronze already buffed to a shiny polish by thousands of small hands before mine. Making a statue *of* a child so accessible *to* a child was a wonderful introduction to statuary. And thinking about it now, this free-spirited youth perched on top of his fantasy woodland anticipated the extraordinary gardens conjured up by the young, playful and

liberated imaginations of Edward James and Frederick Hundertwasser in a jungle and a mangrove swamp.

When I was six we left the oaks of England for the palms of the Riviera and the sun-drenched sensuality of colour and scent. Our pink villa was surrounded by pergolas draped in crimson bougainvillea and green vines, a minute's walk from a turquoise sea. A double row of lemon trees perfumed the garden in winter, and in late summer the high reaches of four old and easily climbed fig trees provided a potent, shaded canopy of large leaves with soft ripe fruit at my fingertips. For this, I am sure Bacchus would have foregone all his grapes, if only he had thought of it. Mimosa and eucalyptus grew wild on the dirt roads. Canny lizards played dead as they basked on the old stone walls but vanished in a flash. The crickets were slower off the mark, and we would crawl through the long grass and tickle their legs with a little twig until they leaped, and all the while what was being released and unconsciously absorbed was the scent of the wild mint, thyme and rocket.

We often went to Paris, and the black dachshund straining at the end of his leash pulled me into the sober world of the Tuileries Gardens. Peter Pan was replaced by lofty French worthies, mounted, to my mind, on very boring plinths. Their blank, expressionless stares were as cold as the marble they were made of. What the statues lacked in warmth, the gardens made up for in the beauty of symmetry. Vistas and perfectly aligned trees offered tranquillity through balance and repetition. Parisian society spilled into this serenity with their children, their dogs, their newspapers and gossip, and that national pastime, perfected in the cafés, of just sitting about, absorbing the atmosphere. The art of doing absolutely nothing is very difficult to practise in one's own garden.

Outside Paris, in a small village near Giverny, lived my great aunt Zélah, who was in her nineties, and over sixty years had fashioned her tiny garden by the banks of the river Epte according to her taste and needs. A scheme of rectangular beds, about the size of Monet's paintbox beds, were planted with irises, roses, dahlias and poppies and other annuals which she used as models to paint from, meticulously, on tiny bits of china, and then embellished with exotic birds. But the most enchanting things about it were the ducks, which paddled freely through the flowers and along the earth paths, and a prevailing sense of *laissez vivre*. It was a garden she was never out of, and you could hardly tell where she ended and the garden began.

All this came to an abrupt end when we moved to Connecticut when I was ten. The clapboard houses had front lawns and sprinklers, just like the movies, and a patio barbecue in the backyard, planted with a random selection of shrubs and trees. The outlying woods, into which I wandered like an innocent looking for wild things, were treacherous with poison ivy, oak and sumac, and the itching and blisters which ensued for weeks during the long hot summers were soothed with enough calamine lotion and wrappings of white gauze to equip me for eternal life in an Egyptian tomb. Absorbed by their country clubs on the weekends, nobody gardened the backyards of this particular street of this particular 1960s American suburb. It was a no-man's-land, with no thought, no plan, no history, no associations and, worst of all, no interest in creating any. Even then I expected gardens to be about something, and these gardens weren't about anything at all. This void, this vacuum, left me with a horror of indifferent gardening and it was then I sowed my first packet of seeds. It would be many years before I realized that the conventions of a culture also inhibit gardeners.

Two years later we moved again, and there was another garden, in rural, pretty north-west Connecticut, with a vast lawn overlooking a lake, and glorious autumn colour, but by then the dachshund had died and I was in boarding school and the day-to-day life that binds one to a garden was over. J. M. Barrie wrote somewhere that 'nothing that happens after we are twelve matters very much', and as far as gardens go, the elements of visual drama, fantasy, symmetry and sensuality which absorb me today had all been planted, and sat more or less dormant until I was twenty-four and marriage handed me a garden of my own. In time, the tendrils of those memories and scents pulled me back to the Riviera, to another painter's garden in Giverny, to Edith Wharton's passion for old Europe as terrain I instinctively understood. But what I learned to treasure most of all was the importance of continuity in a garden.

It had been my dream to make a career in documentaries, but I opted for a life in rural Cumbria, and I started gardening. Inevitably my curiosity was aroused by other people's experiences and, with it, a desire to communicate

...the tendrils of those memories and scents pulled me back to... another painter's garden in Giverny...

this in words and pictures. The images may be static and the voices, typeset on a printed page, are silent; nonetheless they are there, and always for me they are the stories of people's lives and loves expressed in their gardens. Perhaps I would be more interested in plants if I could grow more of them myself, but this is difficult as I live four miles from the wettest spot in England. I learned the hard way to work with a narrow range of plants which sat naturally amongst the wild landscape of the fells, and to love the plants that would grow for me, and then, when I became a garden photographer, grow happily, without me. For the great irony of this *métier* is the sacrifice of your own garden. Just when our gardens are beginning to look like some kind of civilized place, we are invariably in and out of everyone else's.

> I learned the hard way to work with a narrow range of plants which sat naturally amongst the wild landscape of the fells...

A photographer's brief is to give a sense of a garden as a whole, as the sum of its parts; to convey beauty, atmosphere and a sense of unfolding time. But it is the paradox of our craft that a garden is fragmented into a kaleidoscope of images, seized in a split second, and that the reality of a garden does not always meet the criteria for conventional beauty.

It's a bit like the fashion industry. Picture editors, meeting public demand, preside over the grand ballroom of horticultural imagery where the photographer partners the garden in a dance to the dream of perfection. No one wants to see dead flowers on a gloomy afternoon. Yet, as Beth Chatto said as we contemplated the grasses and seed heads in her gravel garden in November, 'There is beauty in decay.' What a writer can make poetic, a photographer is asked to discard. I don't feel I have been entirely truthful about a garden until I have written about it.

When people make their gardens an intimate and integral part of their life, visual eloquence usually follows and the form these gardens take, in terms of planting or design, is always interesting. A Greek village garden comprised of nothing more than a goat, an olive tree and a few herbs sprouting out of recycled olive oil cans is as visually captivating to me as, say, the garden of that doyenne of pared-down chic, Nicole de Vesian, whose simplicity belies its sophistication.

The enduring appeal of a garden is the scope it offers people to express themselves creatively at any level, in any style. This can range from a garden as complex as the subversive, erudite seventeenth-century enigma of Bomarzo, which mocked the mythological iconography of Renaissance gardens made by the vain-glorious cardinals of Rome in their own image, to something as simple as Mrs Holland's witty response to her 1947 wedding featured in the BBC series *Garden Stories*. There she stood in her front garden, between her semi-detached house and the road, somewhere in the north of England, clipping the commemorative pieces of topiary she had planted, trained and maintained, over thirty years, recounting the highlights of her big day. The church was locked when they arrived because the vicar had forgotten about them, and she had to be driven round and round the district until he was found. The photographer charged them a lot of money and then produced only one picture and the groom wasn't even in it. The cake, which she could only pretend to cut because it had been loaned out for another wedding, was made of cardboard and icing sugar. And so, this bride decided she would have her cake, a cake she could cut as much as she liked, and she made one, a tall chunky one, in three tiers of privet on the front lawn of her house, and next to it a basket in topiary, to hold the flowers she never had.

It is the process by which people arrive at the gardens they have made which fascinates me; the sources, references, connections and singular passions that seep into the well of the unconscious and swirl around for years, before ideas for a garden are finally ready to be drawn. Lives are lived, thoughts are thought, and, as George Melly says in his pithy description of Outsider Art, 'You lower a bucket into the mind and see what comes up.' This is particularly true of a garden *Gardens Illustrated* sent me to photograph when it was still was quite young, and it belongs to the conductor and harpsichordist, William Christie.

You could say this garden was first glimpsed in the mind's eye of a child. William began playing Bach when he was five, but there was nothing

connecting the music he was playing inside the house with the acres of mown lawn and big trees of his garden in upstate New York. The American landscape garden reflects the breadth of the American landscape and has more in common with the free, expansive music of Aaron Copland, Bernstein and Ferde Grofé than the precise, disciplined art of the fugue. William's young antenna sensed this when he visited a formal garden in Virginia when he was seven, and he distinctly remembers thinking to himself what you could do with shapes and designs.

By the time he sat down to sketch out on paper the arabesques for the parterre of his first garden, he was forty-three. The lines must have flowed fluently from his pen, because when he conducts, he never uses a baton, but traces out the music with his fingers, shaping and, lately, almost digging the sound out of his orchestra with his hands. It is the music of Purcell, Handel, Monteverdi and Mozart – and of Lully, Rameau and Charpentier, those neglected French composers William rescued from oblivion when he moved to Paris in the early 1970s, to live by his music, and to live surrounded by the art, architecture and gardens created at the time the music was being written.

His passion for the whole aesthetic of the Baroque inspired another act of resurrection; the purchase and restoration of a derelict seventeenth-century bastide, which he bought with the sole purpose of making a garden around it, and to realize 'ideas which had been in my imagination for twenty years'. The structure of Le Bâtiment reflects what was uppermost in his mind at first: a strong pull towards formality, towards the architectural and the sober. In the detail, there are touches of Beatrix Farrand's eclectic garden, Dumbarton Oaks, which fused Arts and Crafts with the Italian style.

References to Baroque opera and music pervade a garden which he perceives as a *clin d'oeil* into an epoch. The laws of proportion and symmetry govern the design of classical gardens as they do the structure of classical music. There is rhythm in the planting, and tempo in the spacing of those plants. The parterre was conceived as a raked stage; the *théâtre de verdure, bosquetto* and cloister garden were drawn from the libretti of Baroque operas where scenes are often set in gardens. Contrast is a key element of the Baroque and you find it here in a counterpointing of light and shade, of large and small spaces; of angular shapes and shapes that turn around on themselves; of sensuality and restraint. What runs throughout is the clarity of its lines.

> ...you find it here in a counterpointing of light and shade...

All this can also be said of his interpretation of the music. A mutual friend remarked that when he hears the music he thinks of the garden. Baroque music, as I remember it, always sounded like notes spinning through air, piped like elevator musak into genteel teashops and improving bookshops. After photographing this garden for the first time, I was curious to hear William's music, and it is music I have grown to love deeply for reasons I hope you will discover for yourself.

The view from the back of the house sweeps across to a hillside William acquired only a few years ago, where he planted a circle of pine trees around a circle of stone slabs. You can barely see it as the trees are young, but it represents the last scene from Lully's opera *Atys* in which the hero Atys is turned into a stone pine. This was an opera William wanted to stage but no one wanted to back, because it hadn't been performed since Lully's death over three hundred years ago. He persevered, it was a huge success and it put Lully back on the musical map.

I was looking at this view not so long ago, peering through yet another window, hoping it would stop raining and the sun would illuminate Atys' circle in the distance. And there it was, like a mirage – everything I had always hoped to find in an American backyard.

The most inspiring thing about gardens for me is the way in which they make people happy. When this pied piper of the new Baroque takes his ensemble, *Les Arts Florissants*, on tour to all parts of the globe, he sits in the aeroplane and dreams about his garden.

Everything in life is transitory, but you will never lose a garden unless you leave it. The best gardens are not showpieces, but cherished, private worlds people make their own. Anna Pavord put this in a nutshell when I arrived to photograph her garden for this book and sensed that permission had been reluctantly given. 'My garden', she said, simply, 'is for me.'

The view of Le Bâtiment garden (left) from the upstairs window at the end of the bastide looks across the border à l'anglaise. *Intended as a sensual foil to the formality of the box parterre, the bed is designed as a pattern of circles, lozenges and triangles, and rhythmically planted with mopheads of standard privet* (Ligustrum), *grey and green santolina, lavender, thyme, rosemary, citrus and strawberries. Oleanders, grown as standards in square jardinières, echo the pattern.*

Lemon trees carry fruit (right) throughout the winter and scent the air with new blossom. The libretti of seventeenth- and eighteenth-century operas include numerous references in the stage décor to ornamental myrtle, pomegranates and citrus, which symbolize exotic luxury.

The split-chestnut fencing (below), which encloses the potager, is associated in William Christie's mind with the wooden instruments used by his orchestra. 'You can't make music out of any old thing. Instruments require enormous care and workmanship'; and so it is with this wood, skilfully made by a local craftsman into the fences that run as a leitmotif through the garden. Here, the pale rose 'Gruss an Aachen' is set off by the dark chestnut surround.

The parterre in front of the house (preceding pages) is set on a slight slant, like a raked stage. The design, loosely based on the Château de Bercy in Caen, reaches out from the centre, in a shape which repeats the musical notation of C clef. The pepperpot yews echo the shape of the urn and, along the long façade, the old vines form an undulating 'green ribbon'.

William's buxom sphinxes (right and far right) invite the eye to contemplate the view from the terrace at the back of the house, which is lined with lime trees. The central axis sweeps out to the top of the distant hill, where Atys' circle has been planted. A mid-nineteenth-century urn stands in the middle of this large parterre, planted with yew hedges clipped into balls, urns and swags.

Strong, simple, yet elegant shapes are the hallmark of this garden. A large hoop of ivy trained on wire mesh encircles a small gurgling fountain (below), where the pigeons like to perch and drink. The sound of their soft cooing fills the terrace.

The Pleasures
of Restraint

by STEPHEN ANDERTON

The 'lyceum' is an architectural abstraction of the terrace at the opposite end of my garden (left). Part anchor to the slope, part bas-relief, part a play on balance and form, it appears different from every angle (see the photograph on page 33), at all times of day and year.

*Y*OUNG GARDENERS
are covetous creatures, and so they should be. They want plants the way some men want lovers, notched up on a bed head. Youth is a period when gardeners have to get to know as many plants as possible, as they would personalities, and add them to their store of experience.

I was the same at twenty-one. With a degree in Drama and Classics, I was sufficiently absorbed by the idea of gardens as designed spaces to find myself studying post-graduate Landscape Design and to be horrified at the relative unimportance of plant knowledge in that discipline. The course tutors were right, and I was

STEPHEN ANDERTON

After spending twenty years working in large private and public gardens and as National Gardens Manager for English Heritage, Stephen Anderton became a full-time writer and broadcaster. Today he is one of the most widely published gardening writers. He is gardening correspondent of The Times *and author of* Rejuvenating a Garden. *When not gardening or putting it into words, he writes and performs wicked cabaret songs about what drives people to be gardeners.* ❧

wrong. You can be an efficient landscape designer with a good knowledge of fifty plants. But if you come to design as a gardener, as I did, then the truth is grim and a wicked disappointment. I felt like a lorry dragging to a halt in the loose gravel of an escape lane. I got out fast, and spent twenty years learning plants, as a professional gardener.

But what a valuable lesson it is to a gardener, to see at an early age that good design depends only partly on plants. It's like being told at twenty that promiscuity is a sin, and that one must forego the pleasures of the flesh. You still do what you must, but at the back of the mind there is the knowledge that this is an indulgence which will come to an end. And so as a gardener, you sow your wild oats. You read the gardening greats and look at many different gardens, and you make notes about the plants you want. You grow them just to get to know them, for the hell of it – to know their foibles and their generosities, and how far you can prune them when they reach middle age, and to understand their root systems as you lay out their corpses for the bonfire.

And then, somewhere round about forty, something happens. You start to see that life is short and that you are never going to get to know all the plants in the world, and that you may as well do something more constructive with those you know and love the best. Then the teacher's wise words come back to you. You see that you are making a garden with your own small selection of plants. Of course you will still go on meeting new plants, and enjoying their company, and even adding a few to your garden. A gardener has to have a social life after all! But you will no longer covet them. You will be your own person in your own garden at last.

One such pivotal moment came to me when I first visited Levens Hall, near Kendal in Cumbria. I don't remember now when it was. Perhaps a day 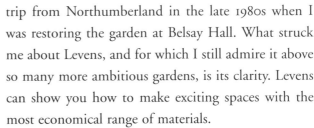 trip from Northumberland in the late 1980s when I was restoring the garden at Belsay Hall. What struck me about Levens, and for which I still admire it above so many more ambitious gardens, is its clarity. Levens can show you how to make exciting spaces with the most economical range of materials.

The topiary garden at Levens must be one of the best-known images of gardens throughout the world. Its rollicking shapes have appeared in hundreds of books in the last fifty years. But the garden itself is much older than that. The park and garden at Levens were laid out by a Frenchman, Guillaume Beaumont, for Colonel James Grahme between 1694 and 1712. Grahme was a local Member of Parliament and had been Privy Purse and Keeper of Buckhounds to King James II since 1685. When James abdicated in 1689, Grahme came home to Levens and brought Monsieur Beaumont with him to design a new garden.

Beaumont's plan for the garden is logical and simple. Wrapping around the grey stone house is a series of compartments, delineated by massive hedges in yew or beech. A high wall separates the garden from the passing road, and on the opposite side of the garden a ha-ha with a large semicircular bastion marks the separation from the parkland.

There is a simplicity to the design which cannot fail to please. On Beaumont's walls were pears and grapes. Within the garden's various compartments were an orchard, a bowling green, a melon ground and a soft fruit area. And it is much the same today. To see the melon and squash walk in autumn, when the foliage has begun to collapse under the frosts and the fruits lie marooned and gasping like vegetable whales, is a lesson in mortality enough to raise an autumnal smile in anybody. Beaumont's hedges today are huge, and head gardener Chris Crowder used to have planking permanently set into the tops of the branch structure to make clipping easier. Chris was the *Blue Peter* gardener on children's television in his youth but is now a family man with children of his own. *Blue Peter* gardeners grow up, too, it seems.

But it is the topiary garden, Beaumont's parterre, which stands out in my mind and in the minds of so many visitors. It is this image which has travelled around the world. What we see now is far removed from Beaumont's intentions. What were once neat, elegant, topiary accents in a formal parterre have taken on a life of their own. They show their years. They have become a motley collection of topiary pieces large and small, each with a different character. Amongst them there are beds of colourful annuals surrounded by neat little box hedges. The bedding is kept simple, usually using one colour in each bed – a mass of glowing mauve *Verbena rigida* or, before rust was such a problem, corn-yellow antirrhinums. It is wonderfully effective and deeply unfashionable.

> They have become a motley collection of topiary pieces large and small, each with a different character.

The topiary garden at Levens was painted by George Samuel Elgood in 1892, and his pictures were reproduced with commentaries by Gertrude Jekyll in a book entitled *Some English Gardens*, of 1904. Elgood's paintings show Levens in a very different mood from either Beaumont's day or our own. By then the topiary had already developed into its cast of characters and new additional topiary pieces had been added, including golden yews. But it is the planting within the beds which is so different. Elgood shows displays of roses, delphiniums, pinks, and *Lupinus arboreus*, all loosely mixed within the beds, in the kind of cottage medley of which Jekyll so approved.

Elgood's paintings were reproduced again in 1988 in *The Painted Garden* by Penelope Hobhouse and Christopher Wood. This latest appearance of Levens under mixed planting prompted a reviewer to remark (as I recall) that the 'perpetrators of the present horrendous bedding schemes at Levens' should 'look hard and long' at Elgood's paintings and 'mend their ways'. Clearly the reviewer was of the Arts and Crafts Jekyllian persuasion, and found no pleasure or meaning in the clean planes of single colours which today are planted at Levens.

To me those planes of colour are the perfect complement to the topiary. In fact in 1904, in the same year as Jekyll's *Some English Gardens*, there was also published *The Topiary Garden* by Curtis and Gibson. W. Gibson was then head gardener at Levens, and took pride in suggesting that the topiary at Levens would benefit from the company of simple masses of bedding, in strong colours, such as blue *Salvia patens* and scarlet *Lobelia cardinalis*. And Gibson's style of planting continues today. What draws me to these masses of single colours is not their shock value, the factor which no doubt offends the Jekyllites. I am drawn to them for their purity and simplicity, because this so complements the topiary. What the Levens topiary garden offers today, in the present phase of its physical development, is an essay in the basic elements of garden design.

Look into one of its busier moments on a sunny day, and look hard at what you see. There are the varied textures of the paths, of neat mown grass or rough grey gravel matching the house. There is the directional pull proposed by the paths as they slide or zigzag amongst the beds, between parallel low hedges of box. There are the clean planes of coloured bedding which cut through the picture at ground level. There are all the varied greens of the topiary itself, in box and yew, and occasionally in brilliant golden yew. Here is the contrast between topiary shapes which hug the conservative rectangle and those which liberally parade the diagonal. There is the contrast between rectilinear shapes and curving organic shapes.

> There are shapes which soar and shapes which hug the earth, and shapes which float suspended on clean trunks.

There are shapes which soar and shapes which hug the earth, and shapes which float suspended on clean trunks. There are shapes which emerge from within other shapes, like symbols of a pagan creation myth. And around everything there is the play of light and shadow made by one shape across the next, and across the colours of the bedding below. And there is balance. What you see is a suite of linear and spatial capriccios, and within a limited palette of plants there is every bit as much variety as there is in a cottage garden medley.

It has to be said that this abstract quality varies. There are more representational moments, made by shapes such as a squirrel, a judge's wig, a lion and a capital B. In some places the linear clarity of the topiary froths over into great swags of scarlet *Tropaeolum speciosum*. These are the more jocular parts of the garden.

But it is the abstract parts which stay in the mind, and which have, in their old age, metamorphosed from an historical relic into a Modernist living garden.

There are gardeners, such as she who advised a return to Elgood's cottage medley, immune to the play of colour and light and shape which Levens represents. I can understand that. To a plantaholic gardener, the Lutyens and Jekyll Arts and Crafts legacy provides the perfect opportunity to collect and mix ever more different plants around a pattern of bold paths and hedges. It is a combination which works. Like George Bernard Shaw's answer for the popularity of marriage – 'it combines the maximum of temptation with the maximum of opportunity.' Only look at some of the photographs of Lutyens' gardens when they were first laid out, at Great Dixter in Sussex or Folly Farm in Berkshire, to see in that generous scale of hard landscaping what an enviable opportunity is there to plant swathes of decoration.

Gardens like Levens are the antidote to Arts and Crafts fuss. Like the simple landscapes of 'Capability' Brown or Humphry Repton, they are examples of a necessary peacefulness, providing us with the contrast which lets us enjoy the fuss of Arts and Crafts gardening. We have had Arts and Crafts fuss in gardens large and small for a hundred years now. Perhaps it is time to let go. Or at least to experiment a little more with the ideas which lie on either side of it.

In my own garden, in flat, dry Essex, I am the first to admit to wanting some fulsome, heavily planted Arts and Crafts borders, places to entertain attractive new plants. Those borders and that kind of gardening I tuck under and around the house. But looking away from the house, in the prospect, I want clarity and simplicity and balance and calm. I want the Levens blend of light and shade and minimalism. It will be achieved, architectural elements apart, by making what would in effect be a clipped landscape garden.

Not having three hundred years to spare, in which my topiary might develop, I have chosen to mix built and planted shapes to make my prospect. The architectural element owes much to Ben Nicholson's great bas-relief at Sutton Place in Surrey. This marble wall is a synthesis of precision and calm, floating at the end of a sunken rectangular garden. What a shame that Sir

Geoffrey Jellicoe, who designed the garden, failed to persuade his client Stanley Seeger to straighten out the swirly 'Dutch' pool which sits in front of the Nicholson. The pool had been created by the previous garden designer at Sutton Place – Gertrude Jekyll. Who else!

It was seeing Nicholson's great landscape 'reflector' that made me feel it held the answer to my garden – the prospect fizzled out under the trees and needed something to turn it back on itself. (Designer Charles Funke has since made a similar 'Nicholson reflector' in his 1999 'Book of Gold' garden at the Chelsea Flower Show, this time getting the pool absolutely straight, and adding a reference to Jellicoe's stepping stones, also at Sutton Place.) I was busy planning my own architectural reflector when I saw Christopher Bradley-Hole's 'Latin Garden' at the Chelsea Show in 1998, which had what was effectively a walk-through version of the kind of bas-relief I had imagined. Christopher designed the final structure for me and, at risk of unbelievable pretentiousness, he lets me call it the lyceum! The excuse is that it is part Aristotelian *loggia*, its proportions based on the golden mean, and part outdoor theatre. Aristotle's beautiful boys exercised in front of his lyceum and my girls lark about in front of mine. So perhaps the name has some excuse.

> Aristotle's beautiful boys exercised in front of his lyceum and my girls lark about in front of mine.

The lyceum sits at the bottom of a gentle slope backed by trees. Its slight elevation above its surroundings marks an arrival on level ground. And leading down to it will be a terminal moraine of topiary shapes, near-spheres of all sizes, which are to be 'sunk' into the turf at different depths. Some have stalled in the open. Others have piled up behind each other, like Hugh Johnson's delicious clipped box 'boulders' in the Japanese garden at Saling Hall a few miles away. Mine are there to give added momentum to the slight slope, to exaggerate the way the lyceum absorbs that momentum and turns it to repose. And they are there to play the Levens game of light and shade as the sun (or the moon) plies its course overhead.

There is no coloured foliage here. All is calm. And the highlights of bright colour are to be found in the bas-relief itself. Do I not miss the gardening, the playing with plants? Well, no. I have that elsewhere, around the house, and in abundance. It is more important for me to have the major space of the garden a calm prospect, a sweet and reasonable space, than to have it heaving with horticulture. I want to give this hundred-year-old obsession with mixed planting a rest (even if only to appreciate it the better), and to enjoy the making of spaces.

Now I can watch the garden, and see the colours and shadows in the lyceum glow with the changing East Anglian light. I can watch the proportions of the architecture and its shadow, and the topiary and its shadow, wax and wane as the minutes move by. I can watch the imprint of leafless cherry branches as they sweep across the lyceum's face. So much of this I owe to Levens, so modern in its reasonableness, and wearing its history so lightly and so productively.

Nature's architecture, in a verbascum (far left), offers a dramatic play of light and shade, but is no more valuable than topiary.

Simple, clean, open space (left) is the necessary antidote to areas of horticultural high jinks in any garden.

Mixed planting is present at Levens (below), but largely kept outside the topiary garden, so both styles can speak their mind without competition.

The melon and squash walk (below) has a marvellously generous, opulent air to it, especially in autumn when the fruits in all their different shapes and colours are heavy and ripe. In a different way to topiary, these fruits are gravity made flesh.

For all its historical presence, Levens is still a developing garden. New areas are planted (below right), but always in a manner which relates to the original formality and symmetry, and with a continuing matrix of clipped shapes, especially in yew.

*This is the kind of moment (overleaf) which makes Levens so special –
the juxtaposition of architectural line and light and shade, over simple
planes of colour. Complexity of line is married to simplicity of planting.
Long may it last.*

Look at the variety of shapes and spaces here (right) – cylinders, pyramids, domes, organic shapes, straight lines, symmetry and asymmetry, single shapes and stacked shapes.

Some may think of this topiary garden as a rather jolly graveyard or a country saleroom packed with heavy chunks of Empire furniture. How can it not appeal to a gardener?

See the way topiary plays with mass, hoisting some shapes to float aloft on clean trunks, and letting others sit firmly upon the earth (left).

For me the more representational shapes are less appealing than the abstract ones, but strength of line and massed colour (below) help to marry them all together.

Innovation by Design

by JOHN BROOKES

*Denmans in West Sussex has a garden which I inherited
more than twenty years ago. Although an enclosed space,
surrounded by flint walls, it is far from the traditional,
for plants are grown in a random way though gravel (left).
The emphasis is on line and shape – Thomas Church was
my mentor.*

I CAME TO THE
craft of gardening
comparatively late in
life and, although I originally
trained in commercial horticulture
– and then served an apprentice-
ship in a Midlands' park department –
it was not until I had a garden of my own, in
mid-life, that my interest reverted to plants and
more specifically to planting design.

For between early training and later estab-
lishment my interest and concern was in garden design alone
– the art of design – on to which I have now grafted some of
the craft of gardening, though modified through a concern
for our native plants and countryside.

JOHN BROOKES

Through his lectures and books, John Brookes is recognized as the voice at the forefront of contemporary design. He is a designer of dynamic living spaces, gardens which are as much for people to enjoy as for plants that thrive in the right conditions. His home at Denmans in Sussex reflects his love of architectural form and foliage. His best-selling books include Room Outside, The Small Garden *and* The Book of Garden Design. ❧

My early garden design education must include Chelsea Flower Show gardens of the early sixties and exploring early Italian Renaissance gardens whose intimacy and warmth I loved, places such as the Villa Medici at Fiesole, the Villa Capponi above Florence and parts of the Villa Gamberaia at Settignano. Large English gardens, I'm afraid, just overwhelmed me, since I was all too aware of a lack of knowledge of their planting content and I had a certain unease at their expression of social status too. I remember being totally in awe on meeting Vita Sackville-West at Sissinghurst once – the garden was lovely, but there was nothing I could say, and that was before I read *the* book. Sissinghurst had little to do with the scale on which *I* lived or the mood of *my* time, I felt. I gained much more from further continental trips to German and Dutch garden exhibitions and just walking round new developments of housing there, I'm afraid.

Quite early I remember visiting some Riviera gardens when on a beach holiday – and the then collapsing Les Colombières imbued a liking for both an abundance of plant material and, I admit, a certain unkempt 'decadence' too! (Happily the gardens are now being restored.)

It is difficult now to imagine the days pre tourism and television, and just how foreign abroad was to a youngster raised in Durham and Northumberland during and after the Second World War. I had been brought up to think of the continent as enemy territory, since my father was a veteran

of the First World War. It was a joy to discover it as the source of so much inspiration in the design field.

My first visit to the US in the seventies was another revelation, and later a trip to the West Coast totally won me over to the Californian lifestyle, where modernity and a relaxed attitude combined to provide the ideal ambience, it seemed. The pearl in the midst of so much expansiveness and sunlight was, for me, a garden by the then legendary Thomas Church.

I had found the Thomas Church book *Gardens are for People* in the London office of Brenda Colvin for whom I worked. It was published in 1955. In it I saw for the first time modernity translated into landscape terms. And it wasn't only the photographs – it contained huge pages (pre-coffee table almost) of clear and simple plans and most of all someone writing in a language I could understand. Our design reading until then seemed to have been restricted to *On the Making of Gardens* by Sir George Sitwell – an excellent book, but not one for an untravelled and uncultured student, I think. There was interesting garden writing by Vita Sackville-West, and later by Lanning Roper and eventually Russell Page's *The Education of a Gardener* – but little on pure design. Tunnard's *Gardens in the Modern Landscape* I had had to find in a second-hand bookstore. Sylvia Crowe's *Garden Design* just caught the mood of the emergent re-interest in post-war private garden design and the development of the town gardener in the late sixties and early seventies.

I was, at the time, fascinated by the paintings of Abstract Expressionists – the Rothkos, de Koonings, even Jackson Pollock – but I couldn't ever see how to use their experience. What was the design logic behind all that colour? James Rose, an early associate of Thomas Church, wrote of Cubist influence, and indeed I had seen illustrations of so-called Cubist pre-war French gardens. Slowly the reality of shape dawned upon me. Gardens were not just for plants, the tradition in which I had been brought up – they could be for pattern too, as well as for people, as Thomas Church had made very clear.

It was the simplicity of the typical Church layout which impressed me so, great strong swooping lines extending the domestic living areas of the typical affluent Californian ranch-type home into its landscape. The concept of outside living was very appealing – and in California in summer of course, pre

> Les Colombières imbued a liking for both an abundance of plant material and, I admit, a certain unkempt 'decadence' too!

air-conditioning, it was vital. In Britain outside living was less imperative, though after experiencing continental summers we began to see a possible relevance here too.

But Church also worked with his surrounding landscape where appropriate. Again the Renaissance tradition in Europe had been of formal enclosed rooms *despite* the landscape in which they sat. I thought of the suffocating intensity, to me, of the plant material at Hidcote, and then the relief of a countryside panorama at the end of it all. And in Church's designs the landscape of vineyard, olive or citrus planting, salt flats or seascape are embraced in his concept.

These designs did not embarrass me by their profusion of plant material – they welcomed me as user and released me as a potential designer from the traditional straight-jacket. They were places in which to play, to relax, to barbecue or sunbathe. Gracious living seemed an age away – and horticultural content too, it has to be said!

The pattern of the traditional garden of gracious living had always been formal and classical in its decoration. Slowly I saw, through Church's designs, how an asymmetrical layout was far more valid to twentieth-century buildings and usership, with cars, swimming pools, drives and oil tanks all being part of the garden scheme. This concept still had a balance, and had a classic simplicity for it was based on an asymmetrical geometry, not upon the golden mean or even the vista as though the viewer is blinkered and can look only in straight lines. Somehow the whole thing had loosened up and Church was applying new rules to his layouts, rules free of the classic restriction where everything had to be balanced, ending in a feature.

Much of this sort of thought had, of course, been voiced at the turn of the century by the early modernists – though rather better. I was only sixty years behind! Nevertheless, I had discovered it for myself.

I later went on to work on an architectural magazine, and could explore this area more extensively. It is still one lacking from a training in garden and landscape design, I fear – so heavily are we into technology on the one hand and the semantics of landscape on the other.

Then came the visit that was one of life's great highs, to Thomas Church's famous Sonoma garden. It must have been sometime in the late eighties. I was

...the swoop of the salt creeks which run through the marshes below, down to the San Pablo Bay thirty miles away.

in the States for something else and a friend in San Francisco, Michael Laurie, with whom I had worked in London previously, but who was currently head of the Landscape School at Berkeley – and who had known Tommy very well – asked me to a conference at which James Rose, Garrett Eckbo and Dan Kiley were to speak. All contemporaries of the, by then, late Thomas Church.

It was the week after the earthquake and to get to Berkeley we had to drive miles round the bay up through Sausalito as the usual bridge had collapsed. The day was curiously disappointing, however. I didn't know what I had expected but these three old gents just reminisced and rambled; nevertheless they were amazing to see *en masse*, and they showed some lovely work, too! Anyway, the following day Mike had laid on a visit to the Dewey-Donnell garden which was commissioned in 1947. The property is called El Novillero, and is located in the Sonoma valley.

First of all, when you think you know a garden from its illustration it is daunting to find that you don't. I knew the house was approached uphill through a park of Californian live oaks – the drive being a mile or so long. The building itself was long and low with great swooping drive shapes interspersed with grass and parking places. At the rear I would see the terrace and semicircular partying area with the famous view, back towards San Francisco.

We had to walk some way up a sloping path which had been created by ground shaping, go round a corner to the left, below the level of the pool area, up some steps and there it was! On a summer morning with the promise of later heat – I couldn't believe it – everything was even more beautiful than portrayed in photographs. The mist was rising up through the live oaks all round the pool, creating a sort of laser-like enclosure to the setting, its sculpture with the lanai or glass pavilion and pool house beyond. Mike went off sketching and left me to sit above the pool house to see the mist slowly lift to reveal the swoop of the salt creeks which run through the marshes below, down to the San Pablo Bay thirty miles away. Their serpentine grace had been the inspiration for the shape of the foreground swimming pool.

I had always thought of a design working out from a structure. At El Novillero it definitely works in from that view, and transforms into a beautifully built shape with a sculpture at its centre. The sculpture, designed by Adeline Kent, separates the swimming pool from an underwater play area, and provides a centre of fun for divers as well, who swim through a hole in the base. A counterpoise is provided by rocks in a grass island, backed by a further mound of rocks from the excavation of the pool.

Tommy Church described this swimming pool as 'freeform' but in fact its radii come out of the proportions of the pool house. (Sunny California it might be, but the bay area can have a cruel climate – at times needing shelter.) I had always meant to try to analyse this design to discover how it worked and have never done so until now. I think that it is quite revealing, and has a definite geometry to its 'free' pattern. In the first sketch you see the serpentine line echoing the salt creeks, with, to the left, the sheltering arms of the retaining walls, encompassing the pool house, reaching out. Kent's sculpture is the full stop which links its shape into the design concept.

In the next drawing I have shown that the serpentine line has a geometry based upon the module of the pool house. The swimming pool's curves echo this geometry as well, although they are not within the module. The lanai for entertaining (seen in the photographs on page 52) is proportionate, too, though being a glass structure its outline floats over the pattern and is not included in my sketches.

'Thomas Church', and here I quote from Michael Laurie in *Great Gardens, Great Designers* (by George Plumptre), 'came to believe that a garden should have no beginning and no end and that it should be pleasing when seen from any angle, not only from the house. Asymmetric lines were used to create greater apparent dimensions. Simplicity of form, line and shape were regarded as more restful to look at and easier to maintain. Central axes were abandoned in favour of a multiplicity of viewpoints, simple planes and flowing lines. Texture and colour, space and form were manipulated in a manner reminiscent of the Cubist painters.'

Yes, that is the subtlety of this garden – it has no beginning or end. And it offers further inspiration because natural forms outside the site influenced the internal ones of the garden – yet the scale, in with out, is harmonious as well. By extending part of the terrace in decking to surround some of the live oaks, they have been included in the layout also. At that time I had never really seen decking used decoratively – it was not considered back home, as wood was extraordinarily expensive then. It has taken nearly forty years to become something of a cliché. It was at this garden too, I think, that I first saw large

In the first sketch you see the serpentine line echoing the salt creeks...

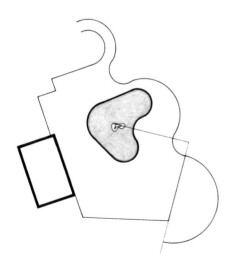

areas of cast concrete, as opposed to pre-cast slabs, which Church had stained a tan colour to reduce glare in the bright sunlight.

Grass creeps in at the edges of the terrace and I heard recently that the frequent watering of it was beginning to have a detrimental effect on some of the live oaks which filter the view, and which in the height of summer provide welcome shade as well. From studying pictures of this sublime garden over the years, you can see that the surrounding vegetation has of course grown and, because of it, the pool is very different in feel from that shown in Church's own book.

It is a credit to the design of the garden that it looks as fresh and innovative and as truly inspirational now as when it was first conceived over fifty years ago, and this, I believe, has something to do with having few plants in it – although the Californian live oaks still provide its frame. For the average planted garden has the fourth dimension of time within its concept. And time means growth.

So much of what is perceived as the 'typical English garden' is based upon planting, much of which is perennial and to a degree, therefore, transitory, too. Sadly, I also think that the Arts and Crafts movement allowed us to get away with too much rusticity in design, which has neither stood the test of time in itself, nor allowed much else to supersede it, so entrenched are we in its nooky romanticism. And there, I think, we in Britain have lost out. For our supremacy in the cultivation of decorative plant material throughout the twentieth century has somehow been at the cost of progression in garden design content. There is a growing interest in the subject, but little on the ground of any real substance.

Yet the craft and science of growing should not be incompatible with the art of design. What we are beginning to experience is 'the garden within its setting', and I think that it is the experience of sites – even if only in illustration – such as that at Sonoma, by the late Thomas Church which have helped to open people's eyes. It certainly did mine all those years ago.

I was later fortunate enough to meet Thomas Church's widow, a charming old lady, living in the home they had shared in San Francisco. It was the clapboard house illustrated on the loose cover of *Gardens are for People*. I really felt then that I had stepped into a thrilling part of garden design history.

In the next drawing I have shown that the serpentine line has a geometry based upon the module of the pool house.

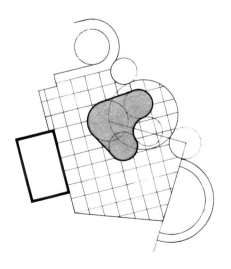

The view at El Novillero from the pool house
(above), looking across the redwood deck
and the terrace to the curvaceous freeform
swimming pool. Beneath the decking,
natural landform was left intact.

The approach to the pool area (right), up wide
steps, to the terrace where you first appreciate
the wonderful sculptural qualities of the whole
complex. The glass lanai, for entertaining,
is shaded by Californian live oaks.

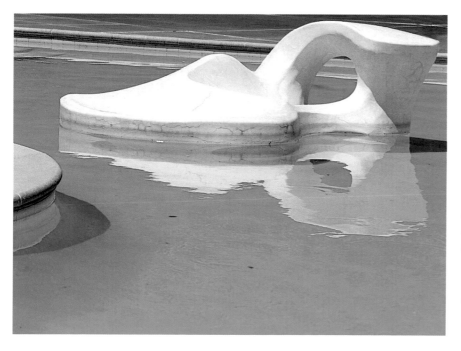

The focal point of the garden is the sculpture by Adeline Kent, its seductive lines echoing those of the pool (above), which in turn repeat the meander of the Sonoma river in the distance.

The sculpture (left) separates the pool's swimming and play areas – you can swim through a hole in the base and sunbathe on the top.

This is the view (overleaf) of the pool in its setting which had captivated me for years in Thomas Church's Gardens are for People. The reality is even more stunning.

A Painter's Palette

by BETH CHATTO

Here (left) is the entrance to my Gravel Garden, showing the value of verticals in lifting the eye above mound-forming plants and shrubs. Allium hollandicum *contrasts with the white broom,* Cytisus multiflorus (C. albus), *while the tall, tiered stems of* Phlomis tuberosa *'Amazone' are repeated in the upright juniper. Even the gatepost contributes.*

MEETING CEDRIC Morris and seeing his garden for the first time

turned my world upside down. Benton End is no more, but Cedric's plants, given so generously to anyone who shared his enthusiasm, live on in many gardens, including mine, bringing him and his enchanted world back to life.

Before I set eyes on the garden at Benton End, my experience of garden plants was typical of anyone growing up during the Second World War. My husband Andrew and I were married in 1943 and inherited the house and garden of his parents. The garden had been laid out in

BETH CHATTO

One of Britain's best-loved gardening gurus, Beth Chatto has made her mark on our gardens through writing about the needs and origins of plants and their role in problematic areas. Her many classic books include Beth Chatto's Gravel Garden. *She holds the RHS Victoria Medal of Honour, an honorary doctorate from Essex University for her services to horticulture and the Garden Writers' Guild Lifetime Achievement Award.* ♣

the thirties, on conventional lines. A smooth expanse of lawn behind the south-facing house was surrounded by deep herbaceous borders. Beyond, a pillared rose walk led into the garden of mixed hybrid tea roses, while lavender hedges indicated the entrance to the vegetable garden. The eastern boundary was marked by a mound several hundred yards long, thickly covered with tall elms and dense scrub. Called 'The Ramparts' it was originally part of the outermost defenses of Roman Colchester.

Our garden soil was chalky boulder clay, left behind when the last great ice sheet, which slid over most of East Anglia, deposited a sticky mixture of clay and chalk (many feet deep), picked up as it ground its way over the chalk hills of Cambridgeshire. In times of drought, this soil set like concrete; in winter it cut like slices of liver, dark with white spots. While Andrew was busy running his fruit orchards seven miles away, as well as studying the ecology of garden plants, my time was spent bringing up our two daughters, learning the arts and crafts of home making and taking over the vegetable garden, since I had been brought up on home-grown vegetables. It took longer to gain the courage and experience to tackle the ornamental garden. (Petrol was still rationed and visiting gardens as a weekend hobby had not been invented.) The plants we inherited in the borders included improved forms of asters, chrysanthemums, delphiniums, lupins and gaillardias, while I went through a youthful phase of growing annuals. I enjoyed several years of larkspur, godetia

and cosmos until I had worked them out of my system. I still enjoy them, but mostly in other people's gardens; although a few, like love-in-a-mist and poppies, I could not be without.

Then, almost fifty years ago, we met Cedric Morris and saw the garden that changed our lives. This is how the meeting came about. Staying with us was a family friend, Nigel Scott. We had spent several holidays with him and his brother, climbing and plant hunting in Corsica and the Dolomites. During the war Nigel had been based on a minesweeper in the Mediterranean. From there he escaped occasionally to spend a few days climbing in the Southern Alps, where his interest in species plants began. We none of us knew Cedric, but Nigel had heard of his garden of rare plants. He rang Benton End and we were invited to tea. Off we went through winding Suffolk lanes between drifts of Queen Anne's lace, innocent of what lay ahead, unaware that this day was a turning point in the lives of us all.

> a tall, lean figure rose immediately, hand outstretched, informal and courteous. This was Sir Cedric Morris, artist-gardener, elegant in crumpled corduroys...

We passed through white barred gates, walked across the gravel yard, knocked on the old wooden door and entered a large barn of a room. Pink-washed walls rising high above us were hung with dramatic paintings of birds, landscapes, flowers and vegetables – it was as if I was seeing colours, textures and shapes for the first time. Filling the centre of the room was a long, well-scrubbed refectory table, and round it a rim of heads turned towards us. From the far end of the table a tall, lean figure rose immediately, hand outstretched, informal and courteous. This was Sir Cedric Morris, artist-gardener, elegant in crumpled corduroys, a soft silk scarf wound round his long neck upon which was tilted a fine head crowned with silver hair. His tanned face creased into a welcoming grin. Without fuss, space was made, three more mugs were found, Cedric poured tea, the conversation resumed. I took a deep breath and listened.

After tea Nigel, Andrew and I were invited into the garden. It was not conventionally designed with carefully selected groups of trees and shrubs creating a background or leading the eye to some premeditated feature or walk. There were surprisingly few trees and shrubs, mostly ancient fruit trees, dotted around. A tall cherry wreathed in ropes of wisteria made the principal feature (sadly, it was all to collapse one night in a wild equinoctial gale). There was an area divided into rectangles by narrow paths, edged by low box hedges, which before Cedric's time might have been a kitchen garden. (Some years later I was pleased to see some of the paths and box hedges disappear and better use made of this space and less time wasted keeping box in good condition.) Other features were pillars of old shrub roses and several huge clumps of the sword-leaved *Yucca gloriosa*. The rest was a bewildering, mind-stretching, eye-widening canvas of colour, textures and shapes, created

primarily with bulbous and herbaceous plants. Later I came to realize it was possibly the finest collection of such plants in the country, but that first afternoon there were far too many unknown plants for me to see them, let alone recognize them.

A few months after that first visit we were not surprised to find Nigel had become part of the household. His youth and enthusiasm were just what Cedric needed at that time. But visits to Benton End were also memorable because of another great character, Arthur Lett-Haines, always called Lett. An introspective and inventive painter, he and Cedric had lived together since the First World War. He ran the household and the East Anglian School of Painting housed in the studios upstairs – and, not least, cooked unforgettable meals. He too gave me a different sense of direction. Initially I was somewhat intimidated by his booming voice and teasing manner, but I was inevitably drawn into his orbit, usually in the kitchen. Here, beside the old Aga, the only form of cooking and heating in the house, I was initiated in the Mediterranean style of cooking, influenced by Elizabeth David who was a friend of Lett. Staying for supper on a cold March evening, I would be sent to collect blanched sea-kale, to prepare for salad by strimming off the tiny pink-stained leaves and crisp, creamy flower buds. Previously I had thrown these away, cooking only the blanched stems, not realizing they were delicious to eat raw.

One day Cedric produced a typewritten, dog-eared catalogue issued by Kathleen Hunter who, immediately after the war, was importing unusual vegetable seeds from the United States. Soon I was growing purple-podded runner beans, a round cucumber called 'Crystal Apple', a little round green squash called Avocadella Marrow, and something called Asparagus Pea, *Lotus tetragonolobus*, worth growing for its name, but needing to be picked when tiny to avoid a mouthful of strings. These were a little taste of changes to come, of many more introductions to our vegetable gardens by enterprising seedsmen. Joy Larkcom, another well-known East Anglian, has pioneered the growing of unusual salads and vegetables and has written extensively of her personal research while travelling on the continent and in China. But she would probably be the first to acknowledge that not all is 'NEW', since she generously gave me the translated edition of a comprehensive book published in 1885, called *The Vegetable Garden*, in which Messrs Vilmorin-Andrieux of Paris describe and illustrate with precise black-and-white drawings the vast range of edible plants grown in the latter half of the nineteenth century.

While writing of Benton End as a garden of inspiration I can sense, wherever he may be, Cedric's shrug of indifference. He did not set himself up as a teacher, either of art or gardening. Since I am not a painter I never heard his comments in the studio, but I can guess they were rarely if ever analytical. We never discussed garden design. Not till after his death did I realize Cedric's garden was an extension of his palette. It was not a planned painting but a collection of colours, shapes and textures emerging and fading with the seasons.

> Cedric's garden was an extension of his palette... a collection of colours, shapes and textures emerging and fading with the seasons.

Whatever *he* may have thought, Cedric inspired many of those fortunate enough to visit his garden. Constance Spry was one of the first, as long ago as the thirties. She would drive back to her London flower shop, her car brimming with tall, translucent seed heads of ornamental rhubarb *(Rheum palmatum* 'Atrosanguineum'), huge cardoons, alliums in flower and seed, and the curious lipped flowers of *Acanthus mollis*. What an effect they must have created, combined with horticulturists' blooms from Covent Garden market! Like many more of Cedric's protégés, she soon was growing these plants in her garden, together with old roses by the basketful and armfuls of *Alchemilla mollis,* which now is a must in every flower arranger's garden. The variety of plant material Constance Spry used in her society arrangements encouraged us to examine roadsides and hedgerows, as well as gardens, with fresh eyes, especially during the ration-book era after the Second World War. Weary of the drab reality of making-do, women yearned for natural beauty in many forms and this, I think, may have led to the birth of the flower club movement. The development of flower clubs over the past half-century has widened tremendously the range of trees, shrubs and plants we grow in our gardens.

Then there was Mary Grierson, world-famous for her botanical illustrations, who still has exhibitions of exquisite watercolours at Spinks in London.

She came to love the plants and garden at Benton End, finding her way there via John Nash's School of Botanical Drawing, which was run for many years at nearby Dedham.

> As we passed through the gates at Benton End into the entrance garden, overshadowed by a huge horse chestnut tree...

As we passed through the gates at Benton End into the entrance garden, overshadowed by a huge horse chestnut tree, among many exciting plants to greet us was *Euphorbia characias* subsp. *wulfenii*. It was completely new to me then, as were most of its relatives now seen in gardens all over the country, popularized to a large extent by flower arrangers who badgered nurseries to stock some of these strangely beautiful 'weeds', alongside chrysanthemums and dahlias. Soon my eyes were opened to an extra-fine form of *E. wulfenii* that had seeded into the gravel, its back pressed against a wall painted warm Suffolk 'pink' which enhanced the glowing yellowy-green flowers packed into large cylindrical heads.

I spent many hours with Cedric in the garden, savouring the plants, where his knowledge and experience flowed as naturally as breathing. I taught myself to propagate from the precious screws of paper full of seed, berries or cuttings Cedric gave me, as well as from his generous earthy bundles of roots, tubers and bulbs. One day when still I could barely recognize half the plants which he and Andrew greeted as old friends, Cedric turned to me with a rueful grin, saying of something that he had forgotten its name. I thought he was pretending, to save my feelings, but now I am much older than he was then, I realize he was being honest. However well we know our plants, the names do tend to drop out of our heads like water through a colander as our memories fail.

Then one winter evening, sitting alone with Cedric and Nigel, I was stunned to hear Cedric say I would never make a good garden where we were living. My heart sank to my boots, while I struggled to assess what this meant. Andrew and I had been pouring ourselves into our garden, battling with chalky boulder clay, but we were still far removed from the ideal we admired in Cedric's garden where no season was boring, where each time we visited we found fresh plants we had not noticed before. (It was practically impossible to take him a plant he did not already possess, although it was a perpetual temptation to try!)

Although uprooting the family, including two teenage daughters, would be hard, both of us came to recognize that Cedric was right. Then we realized we already possessed on the farm at Elmstead Market, right under our feet, the very place to make a garden where we could interpret much of what Andrew's years of studying plants in the wild had taught us. It was an area of wasteland lying on the back end of the farm; just overgrown wasteland, but I loved it. Much of it was pure sand and gravel sloping down to a spring-fed hollow. Once we had bulldozed away banks of blackthorn and bramble, leaving only a few magnificent oaks as features, we found ourselves with a site totally unsuitable for conventional gardening, asking for a series of designs using plants adapted by

nature to different problem areas. We had visions of transforming the poor gravel soil into a Mediterranean-style garden, making leaf-green collections of shade plants beneath the trees and, finally, creating a water garden in the clay-based hollow. It has taken forty years to transform the wilderness.

A large proportion of plants growing in the garden originally came from Cedric but there are some which especially bring him and his garden back to life. For me the alliums do that. Before entering his enchanted world I had allowed some onions in the vegetable garden to run to seed and found them attractive, as well as clumps of tiny chives – whose flowers taste as good as do their leaves, scattered over a summer salad. Cedric had a huge collection of ornamental onions. Almost any month of the growing season he could show me some in flower, from *Allium karataviense* in early spring, like beige-pink tennis balls crouched at ground-level between handsome boat-shaped leaves, to *A. carinatum* subsp. *pulchellum* in autumn, whose dusty-lilac bells dangling on slender stems have now seeded themselves, creating a meadow-like effect

He taught me their musical names, like *Fritillaria pyrenaica...*

through silver carpeting plants in my Gravel Garden.

Throughout May and June I am reminded of Cedric as drifts of globe-shaped heads of *A. hollandicum* (often wrongly sold as *A. aflatunense)* in shades of pink, purple and white rise out of soft mounds of salvia or ballota, creating valuable verticals above bun-like plants. I learnt from him that most ornamental alliums seed freely, but unlike the vegetable onion they can take several years to make a flowering-sized bulb. I am delighted now to see colonies of *A. cristophii*, with gauzy flower heads the size of a small football, among *Linum narbonense* and *Sedum telephium* subsp. *maximum* 'Atropurpureum', all Cedric-plants. But I also learnt from Cedric to remove the ripe seed heads of *Nectaroscordum siculum* (*Allium bulgaricum*) before it seeded. A few accidentals are desirable, creating something more interesting than we might have imagined, but left to itself the lush leaves of this curiously beautiful allium can smother the young foliage of neighbouring plants.

Less showy from a distance, but hypnotic close to, are the many different fritillaries I first came across in Cedric's garden, most of them found in the southern Mediterranean, many of them preferring well-drained sunny situations, unlike our snakeshead fritillary (*Fritillaria meleagris*) which flourishes in low-lying damp meadows. He taught me their musical names, like *Fritillaria pyrenaica, F. pontica, F. acmopetala, F. tuntasia, F. pallidiflora*, referring to mysterious down-cast bells in shades of plum, chestnut brown, lemon-yellow – even sloe black. I marvelled at Cedric's drifts of rare bulbs and asked him how it was done. 'Just scatter the seed' was his simple answer, concealing years of care, first waiting for seedlings to appear followed by fiddly weeding on hands and knees. Those were the days before labour-saving aids like pre-emergence weedkillers. I doubt they could ever play a part in Cedric's style of gardening.

Benton End was a chilly, cavernous place to spend East Anglian winters without central heating, when icy winds blow in from Russia. Cedric normally left before Christmas and travelled south to find warm places to set up his easel, botanizing on the way. One winter, based in Portugal, he was joined by Basil Leng, a friend who was the most knowledgeable plantsman on the French Riviera. As he drove along the north coastal road, Basil, stopping for a picnic, saw a small yellow daffodil unfamiliar to him growing in the short

turf. He gave it to Cedric, saying it would do better in England than in the South of France. As soon as he had a bulb to spare Cedric gave one to me. Over the years we have built up a small stock, naming the bulb *Narcissus* 'Cedric Morris' after asking Basil Leng's consent, which he gave readily. Each year we all look out for the first buds to appear, and can usually pick a few for Christmas Day. It continues to bloom for weeks through the worst of weathers. Its small, lemon-yellow, perfectly formed daffodils with lightly frilled trumpets are a joy to pick with early snowdrops and small leaves of *Arum italicum* subsp. *italicum* 'Marmoratum' in January and February.

Cedric not only grew plants as found in the wild. He was also a skilful hybridizer, especially of Border Iris. He was the first in Britain to produce a pink iris, which was admired by Queen Elizabeth (now the Queen Mother) at the Chelsea Flower Show on the Gold Medal stand of Messrs Wallace and Barr and she allowed it to be named 'Strathmore' after her own home. With his artist's eye, Cedric carefully selected irises from his stock beds for their elegant shape and off-beat colours, giving them names, usually preceded by 'Benton', with romantic associations like 'Benton Damozel' and 'Benton Ophelia'. There were cloudy lilacs, creamy yellows, apricot and peach, sometimes with pale silk petals lightly stitched with fine veins, deepening in tone towards the ruffled edges. But bigger and brighter varieties were to come, new blood introduced from the United States began to fill the show benches, and Cedric, who had no stomach for pot-hunting, retreated back to his species.

> ...best of all I thought, a soft dove-grey threaded with crimson veins.

For many years we watched the results of Cedric's experimentation with the scarlet field poppy, *Papaver rhoeas*. His patience was rewarded. There were many variations, shades of pink, white with a scarlet edge and, best of all I thought, a soft dove-grey threaded with crimson veins. After his death Thompson and Morgan developed the strain, producing double forms. These have been named 'Mother of Pearl'. Thompson and Morgan are offering seed of three named versions of *P. r.* 'Mother of Pearl' and *P. r.* 'Angels' Choir Mixed' (named after Cedric's death). Although *P. r.* 'Cedric Morris' is listed as new, we saw all variants of colour and shade in Cedric's garden more than forty years ago.

Cedric also experimented with oriental poppies; we still have one we named *Papaver orientale* 'Cedric Morris', a greyish-pink enhanced by a purple black blotch at the base of each frilled petal. In recent years we have introduced new hybrids from Germany, developed by Isbert Preussler who for more than twenty-five years was propagator for Helen von Stein Zeppelin of Laufen in the Black Forest. Helen taught me nursery disciplines with German thoroughness and became my friend for twenty years until her death, aged ninety. I mention her because when I first walked into her nursery-garden beneath archways covered with old roses, the floor beneath a jumble of cranesbills, hostas and *Alchemilla mollis*, I immediately felt at home and knew we shared a common language. I was transported back to my first love, Cedric's garden, which for those of us who knew and loved Cedric, is still fresh in our imagination.

The tall, smooth stems of Nectaroscordum siculum (preceding pages) are topped with green pointed papery envelopes which split to release clusters of rose- and cream-tinted bells.

This photograph of Cedric (far left), deep in discussion with three eminent local plantswomen, Miss Hassal, her sister Mrs Lorraine and Dorothy Lowe, was taken by Kurt Hutton of Aldeburgh during the 1940s. Miss Jenny Robinson of Boxford, a well-known iris enthusiast, lent me the picture.

Cedric named this iris (left) 'Benton Sheila', possibly after one of his students who must have been intoxicated by the bewildering variety of plant forms in the garden at Benton End.

This medley of drought-tolerant plants growing in my garden (below) carries me back to Benton End, where I first saw the honey-scented Crambe cordifolia, acid-green euphorbias and velvet-coated candelabra of verbascum. Alliums, daisies and many more came and went in Cedric's theatre of delight.

Breaking the Rules

by NIGEL COLBORN

The laissez-faire *approach rules in my somewhat neglected*
Lincolnshire garden (left), but the planting is not quite as
random as it seems. Along a west-facing wall, yellow and
white spires of Verbascum chaixii *follow on from big*
foxtail lilies, which have been allowed to flop over and,
I hope, will drop fertile seed. The yellow lemon peel clematis
just beginning, and the golden crocosmias which come later,
are part of a strict colour regime which lasts all year.

ON MY FIRST DAY AT boarding school, I was

handed a small blue book in which were printed all the school rules, hundreds of them. Some were logical and sensible, others pointless. Within a week, I had been punished for having both hands in my pockets – as a junior, you were only allowed one – for running through the spacious school grounds, rather than walking, and for having the wrong button done up on my jacket. Within six weeks, I had transgressed extensively enough to be hauled into my housemaster's study. 'Rules are there to be obeyed,' he informed me. 'If they are consistently disregarded, Society will break down.'

NIGEL COLBORN

Broadcaster and writer Nigel Colborn confesses to spending too little time gardening and too much talking about it, but his followers are not clamouring for him to switch priorities. His highly accessible books include Shortcuts to Great Gardens, Annuals and Bedding Plants, The Container Garden *and, most recently,* The Garden Floor.

To hammer home the point, he bent me over his desk and beat me.

A boy with any sense would have conformed thereafter, and probably forged a successful career in the Civil Service or a respectable profession. A boy with true courage would have rebelled, but I was too stubborn for the former and too cowardly for the latter. I developed a grudging compromise with authority, questioning every edict and obeying rules only when they made sense, or when it saved my hide to do so. The child is father of the man, they say, and in late middle age I look back on a life that has been marred – or made, it depends on your point of view – with a compulsion to question everything.

In gardening, as in all other aspects of my life, I have learnt more from heroes who set a shining example of excellence than from authoritative teachers. Such terms as 'correct,' arouse instant suspicion. What is 'correct' rose pruning when there are so many ways to do it? Words like 'great', 'acclaimed' and, even more dangerous, 'respected', when applied to gardens and gardeners – or to any artists, for that matter – are all likely to sow seeds of suspicion in my mind. Who is to judge what makes this garden 'great' or that gardener 'respected'? And the trouble is, when the popular trend is to lavish praise on individuals and their works, the temptation to follow the herd and to abandon analytical thought becomes hard to resist. But resist it one must, if one is to assess true value.

Lancelot 'Capability' Brown's eighteenth-century landscapes, for example, are generally revered, but they bore me rigid. As well as being unoriginal and repetitive, it is probable that Brown ripped out fine formal gardens to create his *faux* Arcadian views. Moving to current times there is, as ever, a coterie of acclaimed designers whose work is not only uninspired, but is also hopelessly out of touch with the pressing needs and problems of our age. Add to them the 'blue fence and decking' buffoons, who view gardens merely as outdoor rooms that can be transformed with a decorative make-over, and you begin to see that the number of designers who set a 'shining example of excellence' are pretty thin on the ground.

Having been thoroughly offensive so far, perhaps this is a good moment for me to admit that my own garden is not merely badly designed – it has no design to speak of at all. Then there is the problem of neglect. I spend too little time actually gardening, and too much writing or broadcasting about it. But these are not the only reasons for the creative paralysis that afflicts me. Far worse, I cannot decide exactly where gardening should be going. And if one's objectives are unclear, inspiration will surely evade.

But perhaps 'inspiration' is the wrong word. Much of my garden has evolved, lately, out of desperation, usually combined with a masochistic sense of humour. You have to laugh, or you might cry! The peril we are in, as humans, is so dire that no one wants to believe it, particularly as the destruction is all our own work. Thermal pollution might enable us to grow mangoes in Inverness, one day, but it could also cause the Gulf Stream to conk out, meaning that our climate will become similar to that of Labrador – eight months per year of sub-zero temperatures.

We live in an age of extinction. Worldwide, we are losing species at an unprecedented and accelerating rate. At home, in the 'developed' world, we face shortages of such resources as water, and – let's hope – a growing intolerance of ecologically damaging practices. For centuries, gardeners have been hell-bent on keeping nature out of their gardens, or, at least, on taming her. In the future, gardens may be among the few places where a little nature can yet survive. My greatest gardening heroes, therefore, are those who create exciting works of art with their plots, but who also enrich their gardens' habitats.

Love of nature in general, and of plants in particular, has always been the strongest driving force for me. Standing eyeball to eyeball with a tall red tulip is one of my first memories – Freudians, no doubt will make something of that! – and I can clearly recall its honey-like scent and silky petals. When I was about five years old, my grandfather showed me how seeds out of a packet could become miraculous living plants and my parents, both keen garden-ers, gave me a small plot to call my own. I was also frequently taken to view other gardens, particularly Kew and Hampton Court.

The London and Wise gardens at Hampton seemed to stretch for ever, and I never connected that rigid formality with what my parents did outdoors at home. But when, as a teenager, I first visited Sissinghurst, I fell instantly in love with its form and style. Here was riotous planting confined within strict patterns. It was spring, and the Cottage Garden particularly thrilled me, having such hot colours, and in such contrast with the cherry blossom and white narcissus in the paddocks. Until I had spotted those controlled colour schemes, I had not realized that a gardener uses flower and foliage as a painter uses pigments.

> ... I had not realized that a gardener uses flower and foliage as a painter uses pigments.

When I started my first garden, Sissinghurst was still a key inspiration. I tried to scale everything down to fit the 25 by 75 foot plot at the back of my terrace cottage but the result looked pretentious. Four moves, a period of travel, marriage, children and a career change followed, but when, in the mid-seventies, the opportunity arose to create another garden, Sissinghurst was still writ large in my design ideas. Then I met John Codrington.

Soon after moving to our present home, we heard that Codrington's gar-den at Stone Cottage, Hambleton in Rutland, was worth a visit when it opened twice a year. Duly, in May, we drove over and within moments I was transfixed. Here was a micro-Sissinghurst – the whole garden was less than an acre – but transmogrified into a glorious mess. Neat, ordered pathways were partly concealed by overhanging trees or shrubs, and yet the order was there. Instead of climbing roses on pergolas, there were swags of colour bursting out of the treetops. Deep in the woodland area, exotic shade-lovers coexisted hap-pily with native jack-by-the-hedge, comfrey and oxlips. We had the impres-sion of wandering round half a dozen acres, barely noticing that we were crossing our own tracks again and again. And in the borders near the house, where more special treasures grew, I noticed that a clump of cow parsley had not merely sown itself among the exotics, but was brazenly in flower. John Codrington had authenticated its presence with a label: *Anthriscus sylvestris*.

He told me, later, that he had spotted a pair of ladies in respectable tweed tut-tutting over the shameful neglect of allowing such a weed to invade his border and had labelled it as an act of defiance.

We became good friends and the better I knew John, the more I admired his approach. His love – and encyclopedic knowledge – of wild flowers gave him a far more tolerant attitude towards alien plantlife in his garden. Dog daisies, for example, ran riot in the twin beds that ran up to his front door and when once I pointed out that he had allowed a dog-rose briar to develop from the stock of one of his hybrid climbers, his response was, 'I know, but its flowers are so pretty!' He once described how, as a subaltern in the First World War, in Belgium, he had planted up fortifications with a mix of the wild oxlips and cuckoo flower which grew abundantly in the vicinity. It was partly to authenticate their camouflage, but the colours, butter yellow and soft mauve, were so perfect together, he explained, that he simply couldn't resist blending them.

When touring my own garden, John was tactful. I could tell, however, that many of my glaring design errors disappointed him and that some of my plant combinations puzzled him. With gentleness, he would question just why I had thought of planting, say, a giant oat right by a gap in the wall, or had placed the pink form of *Viburnum plicatum* in semi-shade, when creamy white flowers might have shown up better. John gave me the courage to let the plants make their own decisions, and to choose their companions. Thanks to him, I've learnt that species which enjoy similar ecologies will almost always look good together, regardless of provenance, even when colours and textures might clash. A natural piece of North American woodland, for example, would boast trilliums and smilacina; in Europe, Solomon's seal and hellebores might occupy the same niche; and in Asia these might be replaced by meconopsis and epimediums. But in a garden, it is easy to bring all these together, like a horticultural melting pot, and to come up with a ravishing woodland garden. And if plenty of our own natives are added – not just

popular plants like bluebells and primroses, but also hedge garlic, figwort, even dog's mercury – then the garden has ecological as well as aesthetic value.

John died suddenly, nearly a decade ago, while packing his case for a Rhine cruise, at the age of 93. But so many of his floral gifts live on in my chaotic garden that I frequently hear his voice: the exquisitely starry-flowered *Smilacina stellata* blooms as I write, and the cream-coloured *Cardamine enneaphylla* and perennial honesty, *Lunaria rediviva*, seed around freely. I miss his kindly guidance, and his company.

Since John Codrington's death, garden design appears either to have gone off its head or to have become even more reactionary and dull. The global ecological crisis is gathering pace and my rebelliousness – call it second childhood, if you like – is getting worse. I cannot see the point in fiddling about with Edwardian pergolas and clipped box when the wild world, as we know it, is almost done for. But at the same time, I cannot contemplate a departure from horticulture into anarchy. Abandoning the garden could turn out to be a greater disservice to wildlife anyway, than trying to adapt cultural practices to suit ecological needs, as well as aesthetic ones. The two must be compatible.

But there's another, possibly more frivolous, reason for my misgivings about *passé* design. Carefully preserved gardens of the past, as well as modern designs in the old style, take themselves too seriously. All those self-conscious rills and scrupulously measured vistas! Then there are the clipped lime alleés, linked rose arches, obelisks – what function can they possibly serve? – endlessly repeated pergolas and those uncomfortable Peto-style water gardens that would look like industrial cooling tanks if they weren't softened up with a few plants. That sort of pomposity was all very well, in the uptight days of Lutyens and Jekyll, when Britannia ruled the waves.

A modern statue of a faceless old lady in a headscarf adds a sinister note...

Today, such gardens are simply not applicable. Everything creative that can be done with them has been done. Or so I thought, until a few years ago I stumbled upon the Old Vicarage at East Ruston in Norfolk. This is a garden

with every classical feature. It has scads of gazebos, clipped hedges by the mile, formal vistas to gladden the heart of the most ardent traditionalist, an Edwardian-style sunk garden and, of course, a posh kitchen garden. And yet, it is utterly original. Daring in most of its concepts, this garden is full of delicious surprises and has a large share of revolutionary ideas as well as the tried and tested; but above all it is a garden that pokes itself in the ribs and has a good laugh. And with so strong a gleam of light at the end of that eternal blasted laburnum tunnel, I have had to revise my views yet again!

The Old Vicarage garden was devised by Alan Gray and Graham Robeson and, though it looks a century old, has been developed over the last two decades. Everything about the site is out of kilter with its Norfolk home. Even the red-brick house looks as though it has been snatched from Edwardian Surrey and popped down among the sugarbeet and turnip fields. On the strictly conventional front, Alan and Graham have created a matrix of classic vistas with hedges that enclose garden rooms with various themes. Nothing new there, then. But the positioning of the topiary, the multiplicity of vistas and a scattering of visual jokes helps to push this garden neatly beyond cliché, into startling originality. The proportions, the carefully evaluated space, the measured pace are all there, just as they are at Hidcote – but the difference is that the garden makes you smile. It's human. And in case you missed the subtler jokes, there are containers burgeoning with outsize plants, huge pampas grasses at the fronts of borders, and the ends of some of the vistas are arresting, rather than predictable. A modern statue of a faceless old lady in a headscarf adds a sinister note to one; borrowed landscapes in the form of several handsome Norfolk Wool Churches serve others, but from one spot, there's a narrow *ausblick* to the Happisburgh lighthouse. For mariners, this is a vitally important structure, but viewed from the garden, it represents a hilariously phallic edifice which, presumably, twinkles at night!

> ...viewed from the garden, it represents a hilariously phallic edifice which, presumably, twinkles at night!

The two areas of Alan's and Graham's work that have given me much inspiration are the Mediterranean retreat and the new American gulch. Both are highly stylized, but both are instantly in tune with conservation issues. The Mediterranean garden comes as a big surprise, entered through a folly, after you leave a green, formal, lawned area. It feels like jumping from the heart of England into the Italian Riviera. There are curved, brick paths on to which spill all the usual bright-leaved, aromatic *maquis* natives – rosemary, French lavender, wall germander and self-seeded drifts of the exquisitely marked milk thistle, *Galactites tomentosa*. The planting is exciting in every season, needs little in the way of water or attention and yet is as beautiful as any part of the garden. In spring there are bulbs to spice up the selection and, later, such self-sown annuals as *Cerinthe major* give a summer bonus. Silver or grey foliage carries the planting safely through winter.

The desert gulch is more disturbing. As their latest project, perhaps this provides an inadvertent reflection of the starkness of our gardening future. A wide area of gravel – not merely pebbles, but huge flint boulders – marks out a serpentine, dry watercourse like a desert *wadi*. Planting is severe, consisting of palms, cordylines and desert plants. The two key man-made features are a sculpture which looks eroded, rather than carved, and a bridge constructed with a series of short planks and slender wedges. Each wedge acts as a keystone, holding the humped shape of the bridge together.

This stark landscape, a desiccated caricature of the classic bridge and stream, is eloquent with a telling symbolism. The bridge's skeletal outline is intended to recall the rib cages of dead animals in the desert. Each component part supports the rest – there is neither nail nor screw to fix, but if one is removed, the whole thing collapses. So it is with our planet's ecology. One species depends on another for survival, even if at first disparate losses seem unrelated. That is why we gardeners carry such a burden of responsibility and perhaps these dry, dead bones of a garden are telling us that our time is near.

Formal hedging and classic topiary abound in the Old Vicarage garden. In some places, boxwood or yew obelisks, bobbles and cubes are grouped to make complex geometric patterns (right), but elsewhere they are used with a much lighter touch, accentuating an eye line, perhaps, or marking a boundary.

paulownia?

The huge leaves of a catalpa (below) – pollarded to make its growth faster and its outline even more dramatic – are laughably out of scale with the cleomes in the foreground of this planting scheme, but which other plant could make so dramatic an architectural statement?

There are plenty of quiet places in the Old Vicarage garden, where planting is subtle and restrained and plants such as ferns (Athyrium filix-femina) are allowed to manifest their individual beauty (left) as naturally as if they were growing in ancient woodland.

Big, bold foliage is a keynote to the planting in this garden. In summer, bananas, cannas and this Tetrapanax papyrifer *(below) grow dramatic leaves in a very short time but, like so many exotics, they need winter protection. The closeness of the sea to East Ruston helps to reduce the severity of night frosts.*

Part of the arid garden (overleaf), where pebbles and boulders play almost as important a role in the design as the plants. Short-term colour is provided by beds of South African Lampranthus, *galtonias and agapanthus which rub shoulders with California poppies – plants from opposite sides of the world but from identical habitats.*

A symbol of the times we live in – the bridge in this arid garden is designed to resemble the stark ribs of an animal skeleton lying in the desert. Planting is sparse here, with palms and succulents, and the foreground statue creates a focal point which is not without menace.

A Garden in its Setting

by Penelope Hobhouse

*Dark yews and hornbeam alleys frame the buildings to
establish my garden's setting in the Dorset countryside (left).
The view to the Coach House, seen across the sky-reflecting
pool, is framed by an avenue of yew cones which, repeated
in the inner walled garden, link the two areas.*

I FIRST VISITED VILLA Chigi Cetinale in 1974 on a pilgrimage to discover Italian gardens, Georgina Masson's book under my arm. At the Castello di Celsa, a few miles further north, and well documented in *Italian Gardens*, I read the brief mention of Villa Cetinale, a mere aside in which Masson compares its situation to that of Celsa in the *bosco* or wild woodland, a setting typical of seventeenth-century Tuscan villas. She described properties surrounded by high walls and forests of dense evergreens and deciduous oaks kept at a distance from the villas by open meadows. Grassy rides radiated through the dense woodland

PENELOPE HOBHOUSE

Garden designs and authoritative books, including Colour in Your Garden, Garden Style *and* Plants in Garden History, *have brought Penelope Hobhouse international acclaim. Among her recent designs are the garden at Walmer Castle for Her Majesty Queen Elizabeth the Queen Mother and a 'country garden' for the RHS at Wisley. She holds the RHS Victoria Medal of Honour and the Garden Writers' Guild Lifetime Achievement Award.* ❧

to prevent robbers approaching unseen in the undergrowth.

We took the brigands' route to Cetinale, following a rough lane through dense woods where wild hellebores (a special Tuscan form, *Helleborus multifidus* subsp. *bocconei*), cyclamen and periwinkle grow in the half light of the verges. Eventually, ancient and dilapidated walls announced arrival at civilization. We passed tall iron gates, encrusted with the Chigi *stemme* of money bags, closed to prevent access to dark overgrown rides, the home of forest deities if not of modern bandits. Our first view of Cetinale was the clock tower looming up, as wood gave way to olive groves and hay meadows. Our next glimpse was of the villa itself, a sleeping princess, high on a shoulder of hill, with an extraordinary axial view to a giant statue of Hercules, symbol of Chigi power, presiding over a deep gorge set in the oaks to the east.

I do not remember how we got in but, except for a solitary haymaker, we found ourselves alone in the deserted garden. We discovered the other side of the villa, the original seventeenth-century entrance which had been the main approach from Siena and there, on the same axis as the vista to Hercules, found ourselves in an alley of ancient cypress. In the afternoon sun, the trees' slender outlines cast a formal rhythm of shadows on the grass and carried one's eye to a building high in the tree-covered slopes above, reached only by a steep stairway. An Italian-type garden of formal box hedges and ill-kept topiary yew surrounded the house on three sides. On a level below the south

façade, a giant wisteria towered above the remains of an English-looking garden, complete with peonies and roses. Breathtaking views stretched as far south as Monte Amiato, where in the fifteenth century the Piccolomini Pope Pius II, the first humanist pope, liked to receive his ambassadors, describing his appreciation of nature in his famous *Commentaries*. And the adjacent almost impenetrable forest hidden beyond the high walls added a note of mystery.

Breathtaking views stretched as far south as Monte Amiato...

We left Cetinale by the more familiar southern approach from Siena and Sovicille and, as we looked back up the hill, the solid square villa, dominating a cluster of village houses, offered a more welcoming domesticity, isolated from the dense woods from which we had emerged a few hours before. Its dramatic setting reminded me of Pliny the Younger's description of the site of his Tuscan villa, chosen for its beauty and the relation of the house to the surrounding landscape. Familiar to Renaissance humanist scholars, Pliny's letters of the first century AD were a major influence on contemporary villa development. And Cetinale seemed a perfect expression of Pliny's ideal: villa, vineyards and olive groves backed by dark woods with distant views of gentle farmland and mountains, a classical Roman garden concept still flourishing two thousand years later. Pliny adds that at his villa, as at Cetinale, the winters were bitterly cold but that in summer the house and garden were refreshed by healthy mountain breezes.

There were so many questions that first still summer afternoon at Cetinale. I knew nothing more about the villa or the Chigi bankers who had created it, but it was love at first sight, a love tempered by awe. Part of its immediate impact may have been the unexpected, but it was also the perfection of the setting: the massive villa with its fantastic double staircase on the beautifully proportioned facade, the enclosed garden with its extraordinary axial views and, even in disarray and neglect, the contrast between the managed landscape and the wild, almost sinister forest from which it had been carved. There are few sites of such magnificence. But I like to think that I was also influenced by the grand seventeenth-century layout, with its long vistas stretching through the forests, almost more French-inspired than typically Italian and emphasizing the east-west axis through the house. These features produced a whole landscape which has become for me the epitome of garden design. The classical Italian garden – probably not original but a nineteenth-century reconstruction of typical Renaissance style – round the villa, staccato trees, lemon pots, topiary and urns to fill cubic space and act as focal points, and the flowery profusion of the hidden English garden below the house, all these provide constant inspiration and confirm for me the value of a strong defined background to garden design and planting. But all the best gardens have an extra quality which is harder to define. A garden may follow all the rules yet lack 'presence' if the setting has been misunderstood. The villa and

gardens at Cetinale work together to dominate the surrounding landscape but the enigmatic woods are a constant reminder of the darker forces of nature which must be respected.

I was already interested in garden history but Cetinale turned interest into a fascination that has grown over the years. The villa, originally a farmhouse, was expanded in 1680 by the great Baroque architect Carlo Fontana, a pupil of Bernini, for Cardinal Flavio Chigi, a nephew of Pope Alexander VII (1655–67), who had spent summers there during his youth. The Sienese Chigi family were bankers, developing their financial empire in fifteenth- and sixteenth-century Rome and employing Giacomo della Porta and Raphael with Baldassare Peruzzi, the architect from Siena, to build their lavish Roman palaces. Peruzzi also built their principal Siena villas, Vicobello and Le Volte Alte, the latter only a few miles from Cetinale. Fontana added a double marble staircase to Cetinale's west facade (the original approach from Siena) and the great door, with above it the Chigi coat of arms, a papal mitre and the keys of the Kingdom of Heaven. On the south side protruding wings were joined by an open *loggia* (later enclosed), and to the east (today the main entrance from the village street) the villa was framed by a chapel, *limonaia* and *fattoria*.

The grandest conception lay to the west where a walled grass alley, in spring studded with anemones, the width of the new double staircase, stretched to a pair of imposing brick gate piers in the niches of which are crammed fifteenth-century copies of figures on Trajan's column in Rome. Today, the alley is flanked by the tall cypresses patterning the grass with long shadows that I found striking on my first visit, but these are not part of the original seventeenth-century plan. Beyond, a narrower alley opens out to an amphitheatre (recently restored with a bust of Napoleon to commemorate his visit here in 1811) where the road from Siena swings round to reveal the perspective view of the villa. Above, the steep steps cut through the thick ilex wood carry the eye to the *romitorio*, a five-storeyed hermitage that was finished in 1713.

The whole seventeenth-century conception of Cetinale had a darker side, which certainly influences my understanding and appreciation of the garden. Cardinal Flavio Chigi not only determined to turn the modest farmhouse into a grand villa but also sought a retreat where he could repent the sins of his youth, making his daily ascent of the steep *scala santa*. In the

...in the niches of which are crammed fifteenth-century copies of figures on Trajan's column in Rome.

words of an English traveller, Joseph Forsyth, who visited in 1800: 'Cetinale, which lies in a wide scraggy oakwood about ten miles from Siena, owes its rise and celebrity to the remorse of an amorous cardinal, who to appease the ghost of a murdered rival, transformed a gloomy cypress [oak] plantation into a penitential retreat, and acted there all the austerities of an Egyptian hermit.' The cardinal named the penitentiary wood the Thebaid in reference to the Egyptian deserts around Thebes in which early Christian hermits took refuge from persecution. Along cleared rides amongst the dark oaks (*Quercus ilex*), he laid out a series of shrines representing the Seven Sorrows of the Virgin interspersed with Baroque statues – mostly by Bartolemeo Mazzuoli – which still mark corners and guide a modern visitor, deep in the forest, along the contours of the hillside.

> ...votive chapels and statues of hermits...make pleasant walks in daylight...

There were few changes during the next two hundred years until, in the early years of the twentieth century, a Chigi marquis had an English mother, a Mrs Elliot, who was responsible for the beginnings of the English-style garden to the south of the villa.

On my return to England, I learned that the Villa Cetinale had been bought by Lord Lambton from the Chigi family and that both the villa and inspirational landscape would be restored and saved for future generations. I have visited fairly frequently over the past twenty-five years and watched Cetinale's revival, accomplished by Lord Lambton and Mrs Ward without destroying its quality and the integrity of its seventeenth-century presence. Box edges are now trim, lemon trees and statues by Mazzuoli sit on their podiums beside the topiary pieces, the amphitheatre at the base of the hill is restored and new formal gardens begin to complete the original late-seventeenth-century plans of Carlo Fontana which had never come to fruition. Recently planted cypresses define the steep steps, the *scala santa,* to the restored hermitage. The woods, whilst retaining their enigma, have been cleared and replanted, opening up the dark *viales* lined with votive chapels and statues of hermits, to make pleasant walks in daylight, while regaining their mystery as dusk falls – not places for lingering in – with wild boar and who knows what else rustling through the fallen leaves. Strange stone sculptures of animals – a tortoise, a winged dragon, a snail and a viper, the insignia

of the various *contrade* of Siena who compete in the famous Palio – also lurk in the undergrowth, evidence of the period between 1690 and 1710 when, because of riots in the city, the actual race was run through the wood.

The English garden has become a glorious reality, embellished by the Lambtons to rank as one of the most beautiful flower gardens in Italy. A giant wisteria overlooks a romantic profusion of roses, peonies and irises which overlie the geometric simplicity of straight lines and right angles, as an extension of a formal Italian garden. In essence it can be compared to the great English gardens conceived during the twentieth century – Hidcote, Sissinghurst and the smaller Tintinhull – gardens in which the bones are Italian, the planting Edwardian and Jekyllian in essence. In the United States the gardens of Filoli, a green oasis in the dry Californian hills south of San Francisco, have the same compartmental Italian feel, an underlying formal control blurred by exuberant planting, rigid geometry softened by planting passions. The sort of gardening I enjoy enhanced by its contrast with nature beyond the garden perimeter.

In my own gardening life, Cetinale, glimpsed in the 1970s, has been a profound influence. In the following years, I visited many more Italian gardens, most of which were constructed more than a hundred years before Cetinale and many of which were more concerned with the manipulation of intimate space around each villa than, as at Cetinale, with long axial views reaching into distant horizons. Strangely, I have found it easier to grasp the Italian 'idea' from villa gardens laid out in the twentieth century as pastiches of Renaissance gardens than from the real thing, sites such as the famous Villa d'Este, the Villa Lante or the Villa Reale at Marlia. Perhaps it is impossible to think with a sixteenth- or seventeenth-century mind? The concept behind a good contemporary restoration or reconstruction can be understood and applied to designing modern gardens. Both La Pietra outside Florence, an Edwardian interpretation of a fifteenth-century garden, and the brilliant Villa La Foce in the south of Tuscany, its gardens designed by Cecil Pinsent for Iris Origo from 1924, are the most stimulating. They were laid out for contemporary twentieth-century life, just as part of Cetinale's established charm lies in its 'living' quality. Even though it has been faithfully restored, it is not a museum: new plants and new ideas give it a vibrancy lacking in the villa gardens fixed in time.

In 1979 I went to live at Tintinhull in Somerset, a National Trust property. There it was my job not to think about design but to enhance the existing layout with restored or new planting schemes. Tintinhull is a small garden laid out as a series of hedged or walled compartments, all squares or rectangles, containing different planting or colour schemes, the main axis centred on the front door of the early-eighteenth-century house. Each of its seven 'rooms' has almost perfect proportions and is a complete garden in itself. Although because of its isolation from its surroundings it has been compared to an Islamic garden, its design origins are certainly Italian, if on a miniature scale. The planting schemes are English – cottage-garden style, much resembling the English garden at Cetinale, straight lines blurred with luxuriant seasonal flowers: peonies, irises, roses and clematis, with two large colour-themed herbaceous or 'mixed' borders and an old-fashioned kitchen garden with vegetables, fruit and sweet peas in rows. There are changes of level with linking steps, avenues of box domes, framed gateways, mirror-image planting, a central reflecting water tank, flanked with grass panels, all planned and executed by Phyllis Reiss during the 1930s and 40s. Tintinhull got into my bones and every garden I design, including my own new one in Dorset, has a bit of something I learned there, a practical expression of an idea.

> it is always Cetinale which hovers at the back of my mind, shining like a beacon...

But it is always Cetinale which hovers at the back of my mind, shining like a beacon on my own efforts at garden design and garden writing. Its unique situation and the mystery of its woods cannot be replicated, so its influence must remain subliminal. We bought our house at Bettiscombe because of its setting, looking out over the Dorset hills that form a background of buff, brown, green and bring welcome relief to the colour and bustle of the inner garden. Perhaps my avenue of yew pillars, which reaches through the hall into the walled garden on the other side of the house, reflects Cetinale's axial views, although on a cottage-garden scale.

Cetinale has an extraordinary presence and atmosphere, a seventeenth-century Italian Baroque garden which seems perfectly adjusted to inspire twenty-first-century thought.

Part of the new garden at Villa Cetinale, still under construction (below).
Box cones frame a bench in the orchard, backed by tall cypress trees,
romantically draped by a Banksian rose.

In the English-style garden below the villa, a stone figure adorning a balustrade (left) is framed by flowers and leaves. Throughout the garden, the planting is a foil to architectural urns and statuary.

Today, in front of the villa (below), lemon trees in pots sit on plinths to complement the Mazzuoli statues and the immaculately clipped box shapes.

Looking towards the hills above Siena from the old approach road (left), the massive Villa Cetinale, embowered by olive groves and protective cypresses, dominates the landscape. The clock tower can be seen on the far left of the photograph.

In spring (overleaf) the grass under the olive trees above the villa is studded with wild flowers, later to provide a hay crop. The whole scene at Cetinale combines formality of garden structure with the relaxed beauty of orchards and the open countryside.

The dramatic view (below) from the double staircase at the back of the villa looks up the cypress alley towards the steep hill and rough steps leading to Cardinal Chigi's romitorio, *recently restored by Lord Lambton.*

One of the features of Cetinale is the gloriously memorable wisteria, probably a hundred years old, which clothes the villa. It dominates the lower garden and fills it with scent. Although the layout here is still quite formal, exuberant planting disguises its geometry to give a distinctive English flavour. After the comparative austerity of the 'green' Italian garden above, in which clipped box, stone statues and lemon trees set a quieter note, this secret garden area comes as a surprise and additional pleasure to the visitor, with colour and fragrance making the perfect complement to textured formality.

Gardens as Theatre

by MARY KEEN

*In my own garden (left), cut totem poles of yew stand
among valerian and rosemary. Below them lies a terrace
with four topiary pillars rising from square bases and set in
grass. This small space echoes the Saxon church behind the
house and leads the eye to the larger green areas of lawn and
valley beyond. Of course, flowers are irresistible. I cannot
live without them. A visit to Piet Oudolf's garden inspired
the planting of* Cirsium rivulare *'Atropurpureum' with*
Allium hollandicium *'Purple Sensation' in the summer
garden, seen in the photograph on page 113.*

*I*T IS THE OTHER-
worldly quality of gardens
that has always appealed
to me. Only in places where
time stands still do you start to feel
that there is something going on
which is more important than the
everyday world. As the small cares fall away, the
focus shifts to what really matters. When
George Eliot talked about the roar that lies on
the other side of silence and Pascal wrote of
being afraid of the silence of space, they were both articulating ideas which most of us cannot express. Beyond their preoccupations with the human condition lies an acceptance of
universal truths. If gardens have meant so much to so many,

MARY KEEN

Garden consultant and a leading garden designer, Mary Keen is an accomplished and highly respected writer. She is a member of the National Trust Gardens Panel. Her sensitivity to the spirit of the place, and her planting knowledge and skill, have earned her numerous private design commissions and prestigious public projects, including gardens around the new Opera House at Glyndebourne in Sussex. She is the author of several successful books, including Creating a Garden, *which features the restoration and transformation of her garden in the Cotswolds, regularly open to groups from all over the world.* ♣

have been the paradigm for paradise, could it be because they form a bridge to the thoughts which we cannot put into words? There is a stillness about the best gardens that connects the soul to ideas beyond our daily scope.

Gardens that belong to the tradition of dream places are the ones that I want, above all, to make. Anyone who has read *The Secret Garden,* or *The Children of Green Knowe,* or *Tom's Midnight Garden* will recognize that trance-inducing sense of anticipation, that sense of being somewhere where anything might happen. Children understand this, but we grow out of dreaming. Getting and spending, we lay waste our powers. Gardens that are open to visitors tend to be arranged to suit spectators, rather than dreamers, and most people's aspirations are about creating something that will look good in a magazine, not somewhere that will *feel* good on a lonely stroll at dawn or dusk. Too many gardeners are preoccupied with plants.

As a child I was sent to be a weekly boarder at a house where the resident children had outgrown their governess. There were about ten of us, in a large old-fashioned place under the Berkshire Downs. I must have been about eight at the time and one summer dawn, for a dare, I let myself out of the house to run outside before we were supposed to get up and dressed for the day. Scared of being caught, I ran full tilt and the dew felt cold on my feet. In the kitchen garden the paths were bordered with rows of pinks and the smell and the sense of being the only person in this ordered place where everything seemed to be

> I lingered, thinking about how the garden had a life of its own, how it went on being there, breathing the scent of flowers, even when there was no one around to enjoy them.

waiting for the sun, made me stop. I picked a pink to prove the dare was done and then I lingered, thinking about how the garden had a life of its own, how it went on being there, breathing the scent of flowers, even when there was no one around to enjoy them. Much later in life, on another early summer morning when I had tiny children and had to get up to them in the night, I glimpsed the garden from the landing window and could not go back to bed. Outside, in the early air by the river Lambourn, I pulled goose grass out of peonies and smelled before-breakfast summer again.

Such intense pleasure is rare and the way we perceive gardens now does not help to recapture that extraordinary magic. In our sophistication we may have forgotten how to make places that haunt the memory. All the places that I remember best and which still have the power to strike an emotional response are not horticultural *tours de force*. The balance between space and enclosure is what matters. And atmosphere. Everything else is incidental. Twenty years ago, Cranborne Manor in Dorset was an enchanted place. Wildflowers grew in the thin chalky grass, and under ancient apple trees lay grey cloaks of dianthus. In the kitchen garden, the narrow path to the church was lined with double daisies. These simple effects and the buildings, a *loggia* with silvered wooden chairs, are the things that remain. The borders were beautiful, but it is not an impression of peonies and roses that hangs in the head. Nan Fairbrother, the landscape architect, used to extol 'the Beauty of One Thing'. There are too many things now, the visual demands in a modern garden are exhausting, such rarities, such ornaments, such decorators' tricks, that space and peace evaporate.

At Hidcote the parts of Lawrence Johnston's garden that I want to 'flash upon that inward eye' are not the old garden by the house with its dramatic topiary shapes and rose-filled beds, nor even the red borders, but the rising view between them that ends in an open iron gate to the sky. I like to summon the wide crossing vista, framed by hedges of daunting proportions, that leads to the landscape beyond and the bathing pool that always seems too big for its yew room. These are compelling images and the Theatre Lawn exerts a strange pull. Any stage suggests that something is about to happen and an outdoor stage adds an edge to the expectancy. At the Villa Marlia near Lucca,

Harlequin and Columbine, stone frozen, stand by their alcoves, waiting for the music to begin. It is a naïve illusion, but it is enough to suggest the mystery that all gardens need. Piet Oudolf's garden at Hummelo in Holland has a more sophisticated theatre. The drama of the yew backdrop to his famous perennial plants is what I remember best from my visit there. Curved blocks of yew, cut with vorticist precision, stand like a series of overlapping wings on a stage. Between their folds are exits and entrances, which give a three-dimensional pattern of light and shade. The plants, for which Piet is most

famous, are interesting, but against this backdrop they become a work of art. Flowers are irresistible, I cannot live without them, but they are not what makes a garden special. The organization of space and the contrasts of light and shade are much more important to me and these I think are the route to that elusive feeling that I want above all to capture.

The empty Theatre Lawn at Hidcote, with the beech trees clustered at the far end, is a good example of this manipulation of space, but here is an added twist to the drama and the way it works on the mind. The group of columnar beeches – sadly, now in their infancy again – touches an old folk memory. All haunts of ancient peace, those places where people have communicated with whatever it is that stops them in their everyday tracks, have strong powers. Thousands of years ago, stone circles and sacred groves were places for worship; they are still places which reek of otherworldliness. Go to the Rollright Stones in Oxfordshire, a miniature Stonehenge, and stand in the centre of the circle, and you may feel the ghosts of ancient feelings swirling through the air. In any wood the sense of being somewhere apart and otherworldly is strong. Reminders of such places in a garden can be similarly disturbing. At Hidcote, where the beeches are set out like a sacred grove, you feel not menace exactly,

but a sense that if you stepped from the space of the lawn into the circle of trees, it would feel different. And yet, all this is at such a subconscious, subliminal level that even as the idea crystallizes into words it vanishes. If any part of a garden can encourage that leap into imaginative territory, that willing suspension of disbelief, which is the prelude to poetry, then it will haunt the memory. I cannot describe how such places are made, but some element of all this can sometimes be recreated, like a faint echo of the place that first made the mind somersault with emotion. This requires intense powers of observation. The longer you stand and stare, the more chance there is that the magic will enter your subconscious, so that it translates into an instinct. When that happens, you find that you know what it is that you want to create. The subconscious memory becomes a touchstone, so that if any distraction creeps in it will immediately seem wrong.

Restraint is important. I think this is something which is achieved not by flowers, but by the spaces between the brightness. There are two places in my garden where I feel what I can only describe as the undertow. Below a steep bank, in a bowl of grass that we call the Dell, there is a circle of mown lawn. The rest is wild. Walking along the top you look down at the banks studded in turn with snowdrops, anemones like fallen patches of sky, then blossom of malus, viburnum and thorn, followed by wild roses and syringas. In autumn, hips and berries hang from the bushes. All year you can go down the grass steps to stand in the mown circle surrounded by this pageant of nature and always I think, '*This* is the part which works.' If I try to analyze what inspired it, the subconscious awareness of the sacred circle, or the space at the centre of the spinning world, it sounds pretentious and until writing this I had never thought about what made me do it. Nor about how the steep-sided man-made banks reminded me of lost places in the Downs or steep combes where wild flowers grow. Nature is always an inspiration.

In another place, on a small terrace not more than three or four yards

> Restraint is important. I think this is something which is achieved not by flowers, but by the spaces between the brightness.

wide and twice as much in length, I came in the end, via several discarded flowerbeds, to topiary. The base plan of a small ruined chapel with an apse and four pillars lies below rocks of rosemary, and green totem poles of cut yew. As an echo of the Saxon church that lies behind the house, it was deliberate. The ordered contrast to the steep bank of rosemary cut into huge boulders below the pagan-looking yews just happened and only now do I begin to wonder whether the change of mood is what makes this area feel special. The inspiration for this is easier to find. Topiary has the power to provide a presence in the garden and, like sculpture, it can prompt the ideas and associations that can create a world with its own identity.

> ...between the narrowest of all openings you emerge to find a green theatre lawn presided over by a disgruntled cherub...

Nowhere is this more effective than at Beckley. If ever there was a place to wander in the mind, it is around that strange, moated, early house that lies in the centre of Otmoor, not far from Oxford. It is a place full of the ghosts of associations. Quite what they might be is never clear. Shapes loom over the next hedge and, through narrow gaps, views open on to tableaux of indefinable shapes. Always disorientated, you retrace a path, only to find a different exit to another unexpected view. It is a hypnotic experience where you can lose yourself, both literally and figuratively. In one part, a double avenue of topiarized yew bulks never match one another. A round looms opposite a square, a pyramid presents to a spiral and then a helter-skelter opposes a dome. Throughout the garden, the scale changes abruptly from giant to pygmy and between the narrowest of all openings you emerge to find a green theatre lawn presided over by a disgruntled cherub. The rhythm of space and enclosure works on the mind like a mantra, while the smell of box rises in the air like incense. Behind the hedges, water laps and the moat curls sleepily round the enchanted garden. Beyond the first band of water lies a green walk, grass green and cool, encircled by another ring of water, and beyond again the flat wild meadows of lonely Otmoor. Beckley lies protected, as though at the heart of a maze, away from every sound and sight of the spinning world outside. It is a place where you feel above all that time stands still, so still, that you might hear the grass growing. Near the house are domestic flowers — roses, hollyhocks, easy things that seem reassuring after so much that is strange. It has everything that a garden needs: a sense of enclosure, changes of

mood and scale, mystery, strong effects as well as domestic places and peace beyond belief.

Creating somewhere like Beckley is not easy. I think it helps to have a strong idea of what a place is about before you start and to make everything else subservient to that one idea, so that nothing jars. With practice this can become an instinct, but the receivers need to be finely tuned and this only comes with years of looking. As a member of the Gardens Panel, I owe an enormous debt of gratitude to the National Trust for teaching me how to see gardens and to understand how different each one can be, especially the green gardens. The temples, grass and water of places like Stowe in Buckinghamshire and Studley Royal, near Ripon, seem dull if they are not properly understood, because their scale and concept is so much larger than anything most of us can manage. Working with clients is also an education. Realizing what they want and what their place is about, not imposing something from outside is difficult. Not everyone wants to listen to the place. They want to garden, rather than make a garden and there is a big difference.

> ...it leaves you free to walk or sit so that your head can be filled with something calmer...

Playing with plants is a lasting pleasure for everyone, partly because it is so colourful that it is fun, and for those of us who enjoy working outside, it is physical enough to anaesthetize the mind. But that is only a small part of a garden. Admiration for a border or for a collection of special plants is like having a pretty dress. Flowers are the outward trappings and I think they can mar as well as make a garden. If they fight the spirit of the place, as so often they do, then everything else is wasted. The real point is the place and what it does to you as a person and how, having drained and smoothed the mind, so that all the worries evaporate, it leaves you free to walk or sit so that your head can be filled with something calmer than the trivia which we all collect in our brains. When people say 'it's got a lovely feeling' about any garden that I make, that is for me the best of all compliments. If this sounds austere, you may not yet have felt the siren call of those extraordinary places which have meant so much to me. As a mood-altering drug, such gardens have no rival. Imagine shade when you are hot, and space when you feel crowded; add to that a sense that nothing else matters except what is here and now, that time has stopped, and all is well with the world and will be so forever.

The house at Beckley stands sideways to the garden of topiary shapes. On either side of the path (top) nothing matches and over the years the clipper's whim has given each bush of yew its own identity.

The bulky bear (above) is almost abstract. A smaller, more representational version might have looked twee but all the bushes are on the grand scale at Beckley.

The moat (right and overleaf) has cool waters that protect Beckley, creating a magic circle at the heart of the flat and lonely fields of Otmoor. All year, water laps and curls sleepily, greenly, around the enchanted garden.

At Beckley the use of scale is arrestingly varied. This garden of old-fashioned roses (right) is domestic in feeling with narrow paths and small features, but the end opens out to a semicircle of green, with a cherub sitting at its centre.

Verticals make any garden seem exciting. The sword-shaped leaves of crocosmia are, in the end, more satisfying than the rose (below). Cut pyramids of yew, like these in the background, look interesting all year.

We worry too much that paths should lead directly to their destination. Too much symmetry makes a garden dull. Focal points, like this small building (left), can seem more mysterious off centre than when they appear at the end of a predictable axis.

Near the house domestic flowers grow. There are delphiniums, roses and lilies among sentinels of box and yew (below). The door to the house can only be reached by negotiating huge bulges of bushes that spread into the path.

Drawn from Nature

by STEPHEN LACEY

Colonies of native water plants introduce a taste of the wild to the frog pond in my town garden (left). The pond is sited near the kitchen window for its bird-watching opportunities. Blue-spiked Camassia leichtlinii *'Electra' is part of a succession of seasonal colour flashes that make up for the lack of kingfishers.*

*I*T IS ONE OF THOSE warm showery April days. I ambushed the heron in the pond again this morning. He hasn't yet registered that the clocks have moved forward to British summer time, so I get downstairs an hour earlier. The garden is filling out. Bronze leaves are expanding among the wild cherry and amelanchier blossom, and there are some scrumptious scents on the air, from osmanthus, viburnum and *Euphorbia mellifera*. I see my young *Magnolia sprengeri* has opened white; it was supposed to be pink.

Home is North Wales and always has been. My childhood was spent by the sea on the island of Anglesey, plugged into

STEPHEN LACEY

One of Gardeners' World*'s most popular presenters, with a keen eye for new trends at home and abroad, Stephen Lacey is an intrepid traveller to gardens all over the world. He is an accomplished writer, with a regular column in the* Daily Telegraph. *His books include* The Startling Jungle, Scent in your Garden *and* Gardens of the National Trust.

the natural world. It was primarily birds and animals that fascinated me, and the more exotic the better. I even spent the odd holiday working in zoos, at Chester and Frankfurt, and for a long time had an aviary at home. I tell you this because it was probably my quest to find parrot-proof plants for it (there are none) that constituted my first gardening venture. But plants and gardens didn't really start to engage me until later, when I had my four years at Oxford, whacking croquet balls down the lawns of Trinity at the taxpayer's expense, and meeting my first black hellebore in the Botanic Garden.

By 1980, when I followed all the other lemmings to London, to work in property investment, I owned at least a semi-reliable car (a secondhand, but rather cool, red Alfa Romeo), so I could start visiting gardens in earnest. Sissinghurst was top of my list. One by one, I had snapped up Vita Sackville-West's little books of collected gardening articles in secondhand bookshops around Oxford. And as I gradually annexed new areas of my parents' garden, and looked for ever more plants to raise from seed and cuttings, Vita had become my chief guru.

Of course, by then the planting at Sissinghurst was more Pamela Schwerdt and Sibylle Kreutzberger, the long-serving Head Gardeners, than Vita, who had been dead eighteen years. But, from its Elizabethan tower to its carpets of creeping thyme, it was as dreamy as I had imagined, and I made many return visits. There was a system whereby you could fill in a stamped, self-addressed postcard at the entrance gate, asking Pam and Sibylle questions, and I still find these now, tucked between the pages of books. 'What's that amazing crimson-black iris in the Rose Garden?' '*Iris chrysographes* var. *rubella* – seed from Jack Drake, Inshriach Nursery, Aviemore.' Off would go my order.

My most blatant crib from Sissinghurst is the laundry copper full of 'Couleur Cardinal' tulips that stands in the middle of my little orchard garden in spring, as it does in Sissinghurst's Cottage Garden. The combination of verdigris copper with blood-red is stunning (as it is with the orange of 'Prinses Irene' tulips); I interplant with gentian-blue *Scilla siberica* 'Spring Beauty' for good measure.

But it was as much the design of Sissinghurst as its planting detail that impressed me. It seemed to offer the perfect blueprint for the dedicated plant accumulator. First, that rigid, formal structure of rooms, straight paths, and yew and box hedging is so strong that the garden keeps its composure year-round, whatever is going on in the borders. This gives you pretty much *carte blanche* to juggle and add to the plant content: the design will hold firm. Second, every border, or section of border, has a peak season, with plants in bloom at the same time grouped together. This makes for real crescendos, which, I had already found out, you don't get by having your flowers dotted about. And third, everywhere has a definite colour scheme. This looks good, and gives you exciting changes of mood, but it also imposes real order and harmony on an otherwise eclectic plant collection. These were all earth-shattering observations for me at that time. Now, I thought, I had gardening well and truly sorted.

Strangely, since it was almost on my Welsh doorstep, I took my sweet time discovering Powis Castle and its even more swashbuckling borders – *Ceanothus impressus* billowing indigo above a gash of blood-red oriental poppies, 'Beauty of Livermere', in June; the massive shrub rose 'Highdownensis' showering vermilion hips over swathes of apricot and orange crocosmias in August. The then Head Gardener, Jimmy Hancock, was (still is, in his retirement) a great experimenter, a talented colourist and an unstoppable talker (a garden tour with him took at least three hours). You never knew what plants and new combinations of plants awaited you, playing against that stupendous

> My most blatant crib from Sissinghurst is the laundry copper full of 'Couleur Cardinal' tulips...

backdrop of red sandstone castle, hanging terraces and sweeping views of hills and valley.

The planting at Powis is more relaxed than at Sissinghurst, and that appealed to me. The tone is set by the monumental yew hedges and specimen yew 'tumps', which bulge with a sense of plump contentment, instead of being pruned to razor-sharp geometry. And likewise in the borders, Jimmy Hancock allowed shrubs to nuzzle up to one another, perennials to flop over the box hedging, and climbers to swoop from the walls, instead of being meticulously lashed back.

My enthusiasm for hot, fiery colours was definitely fuelled by Powis. The spectacle of scarlet-tubed *Fuchsia boliviana* in a basketweave pot, so suave as to make all its cousins look like dolled-up lampshades, or red *Phygelius capensis* grown as a six-foot wall shrub, I immediately reproduced at home. And that quirky tender climber, *Agapetes serpens*, introduced to me by Jimmy, I can see through the porch door as I write, mingling its red-studded tentacles with the last white stars on *Jasminum polyanthum*, and with a woody base like a breaching whale.

Plants, plants, plants. I was now spending every weekend immersed in nurseries and gardens within striking distance of London, as far afield as Beth Chatto's in Essex and the late Margery Fish's at East Lambrook Manor in Somerset (then owned by her nephew), and I was attending all the weekday shows at Vincent Square that the Royal Horticultural Society could come up with. But it wasn't enough. I was beginning to seriously resent my nine-to-five office imprisonment. The worst aspect of it was how little time it gave me in my own garden, which was 180 miles from London, four hours' driving at peak hours. There just weren't enough Bank Holiday weekends. The solution was obvious. I had to make gardening my career. So, I resigned from my job and jumped in with a book, *The Startling Jungle*.

The journalism that followed began to take me to all corners of the gardening world, and it was a shock to discover how big and complex a world it was. One week I would be talking to a specialist in biological pest control and the next to a professional grotto builder. Conversations with people like Sir

Roy Strong and John Sales prompted me to plunge into garden history, while John Brookes, Tim Rees, Brita von Schoenaich and Andrew Wilson kindled in me an unexpected enthusiasm for contemporary garden design and landscape architecture, about which, like most of these other subjects, I realized I knew next to nothing.

In 1993, Tim and Brita invited me with them on a research trip to Germany. It was news to me that any gardening went on in Germany at all, so I was quite ambushed by the quality and originality of what I saw, first in the trial gardens at Weihenstephan and then, even more impressively, in the Westpark, a public park in Munich. The style being pioneered here derived from the deeply ingrained German love of nature and hearty hikes in the mountains, and the belief that nature's rules can be applied to a garden, too. The idea is that if each area in a garden is seen as corresponding to a natural habitat, and you match to it only species and combinations of species that are found in this same habitat in the wild, a community of plants will result that not only looks natural but behaves and interacts naturally, with minimal human input.

The planting in the Westpark, designed by Rosemarie Weisse, was already ten years old in 1993, but because the plants were so well chosen, and the soil had been kept hungry to discourage thuggish activity and unnaturally buxom growth (the main lesson German designers had taken from nature is that the richest plant communities are associated with soils low in nitrogen), hardly any digging, lifting, dividing, staking, watering or feeding had taken place in all these intervening years. Yet here was the best part of an acre, an open gravelly arena fringed by trees and structured by rocks, awash with perennials which, I was told, reached a flowering peak every three to four weeks.

In June, when I first went, bearded irises, in all colours from lemon and purple to cream and copper, were blooming, in the company of hardy violet salvias, blue flax, yellow phlomis, lime-green *Euphorbia seguieriana* subsp. *niciciana* and magenta *Allium rosenbachianum*. Nothing was artificially clumped or tiered, rather all the plants were mingled and repeated, as in a meadow, and this mood was enhanced by the matrix of wispy, clump-forming grasses in which everything was set. On subsequent visits later in the season, I remember crimson *Allium sphaerocephalon* bobbing through catmint and *Pennisetum orientale*; a blaze of yellow, orange and red daylilies in front of violet

Campanula lactiflora; and pools of *Aster amellus* varieties between *Sedum* 'Herbstfreude' and the tall, red-tinted grass *Andropogon gerardii*.

These scenes seemed to connect so well to the mood of the time. They were plant rich but less formal and more environmentally aware. Among gardeners, there was now great interest in simpler effects – foliage, seed heads, grasses – and in maintenance terms, even I was finding the Sissinghurst/Powis formula hard to sustain, without those gardens' attendant staff.

By the beginning of the 1990s, I was going to the United States almost every year on lecture tours, and able to tap more fully into the story of modern architecture and contemporary garden design, from Frank Lloyd Wright's Fallingwater in the Pennsylvania woods, to Isabelle Greene's Valentine Garden overlooking the ocean at Montecito, California. The last, on terraces below a stark white box of a house, is planted in a way which its designer calls 'museum placement', with each species of agave, aloe, eucalyptus or fruit tree isolated, by gravel or low ground cover, in order to emphasize its sculptural outline and the shadows cast on the stucco walls. It was fascinating to see a garden that is such a complete antithesis of the English cottage garden jumble.

This sort of minimalist picture would never have engaged me ten years earlier, but the more gardens I was seeing, the more I was coming to appreciate what the great designers call 'a sense of place', that element that distinguishes a garden from the pack and makes it memorable. Minimalism cuts to the quick, removing all extraneous clutter, and when it is done well (done badly, it can be like sensual deprivation), the sense of place can be very powerful indeed.

But for the fullest encounter with a garden, it has to do more than please you visually. It has to bowl you over emotionally. And why some gardens do, and some don't, is a bit of a puzzle. Perhaps childhood associations have something to do with it, for in my case, wet west-coast gardens are much the likeliest to get under my skin. Sure, I can be poleaxed by the beauty of the dry Mediterranean, the Australian outback (excellent parrots), or the desert garden in the Huntingdon Botanic Garden in Los Angeles, but they never stir me like a lush, wet Cornish valley or a rainforest.

The Bloedel Reserve, in the high rainfall climate of Bainbridge Island west of Seattle, fits the bill perfectly. Prentice Bloedel was one of the great

> I was coming to appreciate what the great designers call 'a sense of place'...

lumber barons of the Pacific North-West, but he wore a different hat in the grounds around his château overlooking Puget Sound, which he developed from 1950 onwards. The result is a green, meandering garden of lawns, pools and trees, built into a framework of some 80 acres of forest, which, in this part of the world, means predominantly Douglas fir, hemlock and western red cedar, with a damp understorey of evergreen sword ferns and mosses.

So it is a shadowy and peaceful place, and because you have to make an appointment to visit, and numbers are restricted, it is never swarming with people. During my visit, the silence was broken only by some rude parps on what sounded like a wind instrument: we tracked the noise to a pair of trumpeter swans living up to their name. The two formal areas within the garden simply reinforce the tranquillity, for one is a hedged room containing only a long, rectangular reflection pool, designed by Thomas Church, and the other is a contemplative Japanese and Zen garden. The entrance path to this latter garden is lined with grey cobbles and two huge fat rugs of black lily turf (*Ophiopogon planiscapus* 'Nigrescens'), which is obviously delighting in the high rainfall. It contrasts well with the lime-green moss carpets receding into the forest.

But elsewhere, what is going in the garden is really a restrained blend of woodland shrubs, perennials and bulbs, ornamentals interspersed with natives, and all anchored in the natural leaf litter and moss, so that it is often hard to tell what is the work of nature and what of man. Ferns, fallen branches and stumps are taken out where they are not wanted, but otherwise left. This is a composition that seems to have grown out of its setting, inspired by its forested landscape and its wet climate; nature distilled, edited and enhanced; and hugely atmospheric.

All that's missing is red-blooded plantsmanship. So, enter Portmeirion, whose woods take me to as near nirvana as any garden can. I discovered them one May evening, only a few years ago, when my mother took a holiday cottage among the belltowers and cupolas of this fantasy Italianate village, created by Sir Clough Williams-Ellis, self-styled 'architect errant', from the mid 1920s. It is a fabulous spot here on the west coast of Wales, overlooking a tidal estuary, and, thanks to the warm Gulf Stream water, almost frost-free. But from a previous visit, to the village only, I associated the place with mophead hydrangeas, some awful bedding and the stench of chip oil.

What a difference a day makes. This time, the village was lily-scented, heavy and spicy-sweet, from an array of white, wide-trumpeted, tender rhododendrons growing in pots, and stood out beside gateways and on steps. 'Fragrantissimum' I knew, but who had heard of 'Sesterianum', 'Logan Early' or 'Harry Tagg'? Clearly, there was a plantsman at work. It proved to be Dr Philip Brown, who subsequently gave me rooted cuttings of all these scented varieties. And what rewarding plants they are for a cool greenhouse or porch.

Eventually, I spotted a path out of the village into the woods which my mother, who had got here a day earlier, had already alerted me to. These turned out to comprise acres upon acres of rocky out-crops, lakes, streams and gulleys, projecting out to sea. The shel-ter belts, and many of the specimen trees and shrubs, date back to Victorian and Edwardian times. And since this was the heyday of the rhododendron, there are now some monsters about. The groves of 'Cornish Red' (now correctly, *R. Smithii* Group), alive with bees, are so tall that you don't see the flowers until they drop to the ground.

So, enter Portmeirion, whose woods take me to as near nirvana as any garden can.

This is what everyone imagines a Himalayan forest to be like, an exotic wilderness full of floral ambush. Weaving through the leaf litter, and ducking under the branches, you get little idea what you are going to meet next in the shadows: *Magnolia campbellii* in full flush, a soaring *Rhododendron arboreum* glowing blood-red. And here and there you step out of Asia into a sun-lit glade of yellow acacias, or a little swamp of gunnera.

Over the past twenty years, Philip Brown has been developing the natur-alistic theme in wonderful ways, inspired by his visit to Yunnan. So you now meet rhododendrons like 'Saffron Queen' clinging for dear life to steep rock faces among mossy boulders, and dells of huge-leaved *R. sinogrande* hybrids wedged between knolls colonized by ferns and rough woodland grasses. Red-berried skimmias are arranged in scattered drifts up bare slopes; weirdly exotic perennials like *Fascicularia bicolor* sprout from high rock ledges; and ground-cover plants filter at will among native wildflowers. Everything he plants looks as if it has seeded itself just where it wants to be.

This is a planting style drawn from nature, steeped in local character, and less demanding in maintenance, but still with all the luscious, theatrical qual-ity of a Sissinghurst or a Powis border. This has to be the way forward for the home gardener, too, don't you think?

The village of Portmeirion (left), comprising an assortment of architectural salvage and flights of fancy, occupies a sheltered spot between Portmadog and the Snowdonia mountains. The climate is mild, moist and often sunny.

Quirkily clipped evergreens (above) add to the architectural entertainments of the village, which are also echoed in the woods (below). These stretch seawards, west along the peninsula.

The green, unmanicured woodland fosters a sense of exploration and discovery. One twist in a path might reveal a rich concoction of rhododendron and azalea colours and scents *(preceding pages)*, another a solitary eruption, such as from a blood-red form of Rhododendron arboreum *(right)*.

Descending under bare cliffs and past sinuous lakes, you come to a lush, damp gulley *(below)*. Here, the stone arch and wall have prompted a more obviously structured planting of contrasting leaves, featuring tree ferns and giant Gunnera manicata.

Another red rhododendron (left) is casually partnered with the white flowers and tiered branches of Viburnum plicatum. *Later in summer, there will be many pools of similar bracts and lacecaps, as the woods become flooded with white and blue hydrangeas.*

The thuggish behaviour of purple Rhododendron ponticum, *introduced in the Victorian era, has been one of the gardeners' chief headaches, and gradually it is being eliminated. This old grove of 'Cornish Red', a form of* R. arboreum *(below), is a happier legacy, and splendidly mysterious.*

Creative
Excitement

by CHRISTOPHER LLOYD

*The exotic garden at Great Dixter (left) has the formal
structure of Lutyens' original rose garden but its planting
has been transformed into a jungle of bold foliage and
vibrant colour for a few months each summer and autumn.
The deep mauve* Verbena bonariensis *is a running theme
throughout.*

*A*BSORBED AS WE may be by our own gardens, there is a limit to the number of ideas that we can work out in them. We need to refuel on other people's, whose may be entirely different. That is a healthy experience, whether directly relevant to our own gardening or not. Very often not, in my case, and it is refreshing to be able to recharge my batteries on other people's achievements. I wrote *Other People's Gardens*, so as to be able to externalize my own obsession. To get away from myself, so to speak.

Although most gardeners are copying one another or some imagined glory of the past, all sorts of gardens can be

CHRISTOPHER LLOYD

At his home at Great Dixter in East Sussex, Christopher Lloyd has developed the brilliant garden so admired by countless visitors and television viewers. He has a reputation for being 'the best-informed, liveliest, most worthwhile writer of our time'. He writes weekly columns for Country Life *and* The Guardian *and is the author of a string of best-selling classics, including* The Well-Tempered Garden, Gardener Cook *and* Colour for Adventurous Gardeners. *He holds the OBE, the RHS Victoria Medal of Honour and the Garden Writers' Guild Lifetime Achievement Award.* ❧

inspirational. In that made by Charles Jencks and Maggie Keswick, in the south of Scotland, a new landscape of hills, ridges and both still and flowing water has been created and you wish that it extended as far as the distant horizon, perhaps concluding with an eyecatcher, eighteenth-century style. Without a flower in sight, it is tremendously satisfying.

At Mapperton House in Dorset, a jewel has been set in the forehead of a charming, even cosy landscape, where cattle graze and are enclosed by the finest (and most expensive) post-and-railing fences. Within this setting, you suddenly, over a brow, find yourself looking down into a little valley with a formal garden of topiary, channelled water and weathered statuary. There are plants, too, but they are subservient to the design, which is entirely restful, yet curiously exciting also. All gardens should engender feelings of excitement, and this is the reflection of their owners' creativity. There is no such thing as a natural garden and that is nothing to be ashamed of.

Perhaps the most inspirational garden that I have seen of recent years – and it was started only in 1991, which is recent by gardening standards (they say that twenty-five years are needed for a garden to mature) – is Crech ar Pape, in the very north of Brittany. The owners, Timothy and Isabelle Vaughan, met during their horticultural training in England and both are highly professional gardeners. They combine knowledge, through experience, of how to grow plants well – there is assured evidence of the kind of plants

they like so that these can, when desirable, be repeated to carry a sense of unity – with an individuality in their treatment of shrubs which underlines a personal concept of the way they would like their garden to look. This discipline is blended with freedom.

The garden lies around the Vaughans' family home, a series of converted old farm buildings. They are only just above the coast, with the view of a bay in which there are extraordinary granite outcrops. The climate is mild – very similar to Cornwall's, in fact, with little frost but furious winds. For this reason, Timothy reckons not to bother much about a spring garden – spring-flowering trees and shrubs like magnolias get hopelessly battered. But I first visited in October and although you could see that many flowering plants had finished, the garden seemed utterly contented in its completeness at that late season. My more recent visit was in July, when flowers were at their peak, as they are in my own. But there were no annuals, because these entail too much behind-the-scenes work.

Initially, the site was fully exposed; anyone curious (and there are plenty such) could stare into it from neighbouring fields. So shelter, as also from wind, was the first requisite. The shelter plants, of which bay laurel is a principal, have been allowed to grow freely and the whole garden is fully enclosed. It now has a private, intimate feel and, as it is only occasionally opened to the public and then by special request, plants can spill out from the borders and self-sow freely. 'It happens in all the best gardens,' says Timothy. The paths, all paved with granite sets, are a generous six feet wide. There are virtually no grass lawns.

It is a quite formally laid out garden, on a slope and divided into three main sections, these being linked by a straight path which offers vistas. Timothy likes topiary, but felt it wouldn't be appropriate here. Instead he shapes many of his shrubs into mounds of varying heights, colours and textures. Most, except the smallest-leaved and twiggiest (which he shears), he prunes with secateurs, finding this exercise therapeutic.

Among these shrubs I was impressed by the grey New Zealander, *Leptospermum lanigerum.* Also by an evergreen oak, *Quercus phillyreoides* from Japan. It can be kept quite small and is first trimmed, with secateurs, in late April. The young shoots are red and a later trimming produces a second crop of these. The climate suits many hebes and *Hebe parviflora* var. *angustifolia,* after being smothered in small white, spikelets in July, is secateur-trimmed and yields a smaller second flowering in the autumn.

Osmanthus heterophyllus 'Variegatus' has small, holly-like leaves with telling white marginal variegation. Both *Elaeagnus* × *ebbingei* and *E.* × *e.* 'Gilt Edge' are kept in pretty strict order, being large and vigorous shrubs, but this does not prevent them filling the air with delicious scent from their otherwise unremarkable blossom in autumn.

Yet by no means all the shrubs are trimmed during their growing season. *Lavatera* 'Barnsley' (blush with a darker eye) makes a huge, long-flowering shrub in the course of a few months, while the glaucous-leaved, big white

...plants can spill out from the borders and self-sow freely.

'tree' poppy, *Romneya coulteri*, from being cut to the ground in winter, will grow to ten feet in a season. The mallow has the pink-flowered *Hebe* 'Great Orme' by its side and behind them is a splendid, free-standing specimen of *Magnolia grandiflora* 'Caradeuc', which produces its creamy, lemon-scented blooms over a long season. Fergus Garrett (who was with me) observed that its buds looked like bullets. The leaves are rusty-iron-tinted on their undersides.

Ilex aquifolium 'Hascombensis' is a small-leaved holly with a naturally fastigiate habit so that it makes a natural spire without need of any pruning. Four of these, in a formal planting, were each surrounded by a three-foot-tall square plinth of box. Box features importantly in this garden and there are many box balls to give plant structure but they are generally interwoven with soft plant material. The box is clipped February–March, just as growth is being renewed; then again in late July but not in autumn, as you see in so many gardens. That inevitably results in a browning of all the cut leaf edges, which looks unsightly right through the winter.

So far, it might seem that Timothy is more interested in structure than in plants and flowers for their own sake and this concept might be reinforced by the design of the top, round garden in the shape of a Celtic cross (you might need to be told this before you appreciated it). But flowering and foliage plants are, in fact, of the utmost importance, Timothy being a mad-keen plantsman. Yet he is constantly aware that plants must look effective in their setting.

The garden's most grown plants are agapanthus – all either white or in some shade of blue, of course, but of varying heights, flower sizes and intensity of colouring and in many situations, sometimes dictated by self-sowns. The central bed in the round garden is devoted to blue and white agapanthus, which were at their peak in July. The seed heads are agreeable later on but you do, in places, become aware of the plants' masses of strap leaves being a trifle boorish. Certain combinations are particularly satisfying. For instance, blue agapanthus with the cream spikes of the dwarf *Kniphofia* 'Little Maid'. You need to be critical and selective when deciding which hemerocallis to grow, seeing that the choice is vast. 'So Lovely', despite its saccharine-sweet name, is a good one with large, wide-open lemon-yellow flowers held well above the

> The garden's most grown plants are agapanthus ...of varying heights, flower sizes and intensity of colouring...

foliage. That looked good with blue agapanthus, as also did *Lysimachia ciliata* 'Firecracker', threading its way through blue agapanthus clumps. The lysimachia has cool yellow blossom set off by purple foliage. It is a great thug, with its running rootstock, and needs to be brought to heel pretty well every year.

The Vaughans are good at repetition without regimentation. Thus, in one double border in the middle section, where there is a concentration of pink flowers, the brilliant magenta, long-flowering cranesbill, *Geranium × riversleaianum* 'Russell Prichard', spills out over the path in pools of colour, mitigated by its grey-green foliage. There is a purple penstemon and the pink 'Evelyn', of upright habit and small, narrow tubes. The clear pink hybrid verbena 'Silver Anne' is here and self-sowing, prostrate *Persicaria capitata*, whose endlessly produced little globes of pink flowers are set off by foliage with a purple boomerang-shaped stripe across each leaf. In most of our gardens this is tender and needs to be confined to greenhouse benches or to hanging baskets for the summer.

In late summer and autumn, there are the platform heads of *Sedum* 'Herbstfreude' (Autumn Joy) here and of the brighter, cleaner pink *S. spectabile*, though Timothy says he even prefers its pale green buds before they open. There is a wavy and interrupted line of *Aster lateriflorus* 'Horizontalis', at its peak in October but with a long run-up; a sturdy habit to not more than three feet, small, purplish leaves and countless purple-centred daisies in which the near-white rays are laid back a little.

Something deserves to be said about the many low-growing, summer-flowering perennials which are normally, in England, treated as tender bedding plants, not just because of their lack of winter hardiness but because rejuvenated plants raised from autumn-struck cuttings are sometimes (not always) more persistently flowering than old stock. In Brittany you have a choice. Allowed to overwinter, they often produce a huge wealth of blossom as early as May. But then, if they run out of steam, you have to rid yourself of old stock and bring in the new. Gazanias are like this, as are other South African daisies such as osteospermums and argyranthemums. Also the low, spready verbenas, of which 'Silver Anne' was an example. The mauve 'La France' is here, eye-searing pink 'Sissinghurst' and, in the round garden, the little ground-hugging *Verbena peruviana*, which is pure scarlet.

The Vaughans go in for a certain amount of colour theming but it is far from obsessive. The top garden has an emphasis on red, the middle garden on pink and the lowest, especially in autumn, on yellow – lots of brilliant as well as cool yellows.

This lowest garden is the most exciting of all. You approach it through a quite narrow passageway from above and it is an arena all spread out before you with buildings on three sides. The lowest point suggests a pond but it is dry and planted right to the bottom. The planting is ebullient with plants splashing out on to steps wherever you look. In October it is vital with the dazzling yellows of *Euryops chrysanthemoides*, a soft shrub with lustrous green leaves and yellow daisies at their most prolific then; and with *Senna* (formerly *Cassia*) *corymbosa*. This is a vigorous, scandent shrub, which is cut hard back, almost to the ground, each spring but is up to the top of the house by now. Tender for most of us, alas! It is leguminous, with pinnate leaves and panicles of sizeable pea flowers of great distinction. Next to this and either side of a doorway leading into the dining room are wreathing climbers, the evergreen *Trachelospermum jasminoides*, with buff-yellow, jasmine-like and powerfully fragrant blossom.

Another climber whose appearance, rather than any scent, has caused it to be compared with jasmine is *Solanum jasminoides*. It grows and flowers with particular abundance in autumn up a south-facing chimneystack. English gardens grow its pure white form (against the barn at Dixter it makes a striking feature through most of the second half of the year) and I have pooh-poohed the skimmed-milk type-plant. But they have a beauty at Crech ar Pape, with distinctly larger flowers than normal. I was allowed cuttings.

In July, the main source of yellow through the lower garden is from *Anthemis tinctoria*, mostly in fairly pale shades. Foliage, as everywhere else, is of even greater importance than flowers. Grey is represented by *Artemisia* 'Powis Castle' and by *A. alba* 'Canescens' (*A. canescens*), with narrow, wire-netting leaves. The yellow-variegated sage, *Salvia officinalis* 'Icterina', is rather improved than otherwise by the occasional branch that has reverted to plain green. The even stronger-growing *S. o.* 'Berggarten' both here and elsewhere is as handsome as I have seen it. There are phormiums (New Zealand flax), a purple-leaved *Cordyline australis* high up in the furthest corner, masses of self-sowing *Euphorbia mellifera*, which is best as a vigorously shrubby foliage plant, in youth. On flowering, the honey scent is overwhelming but after that it is often a good plan to start again, rather than attempt to rejuvenate the flowered specimen. There is a well-sited fountain of *Miscanthus sinensis* 'Variegatus', with white marginal stripes. In the bottom of the dry 'pond', the yellow-variegated, foot-high grass, *Hakonechloa macra* 'Aureola', gets better and better throughout its long growing season and finally flowers in autumn. It is much represented in other parts of the garden. Less often seen, yet valued here, is *H. macra*, the unvariegated species itself, three feet tall and arching gracefully in the wind.

This lower garden seems particularly sunlit and happy. In one corner a narrow passage leads to the garden's boundary overlooking the bay. Defensive shrub planting (though a large patch of agapanthus among them is surprisingly well integrated) is kept low enough to allow a view of the coast over its top. Here there is an evergreen ceanothus, blue-flowered in spring; the blue-grey, shrubby *Atriplex halimus*, never happier than on the coast; an Australian bottlebrush, *Callistemon*, the white-margined *Rhamnus alaternus* 'Argenteovariegata' cut into a mound, and the pale yellow, April-flowering broom, *Cytisus* × *praecox* 'Warminster', with its young stems (you prune immediately after flowering) in swirls. All these are good windbreak plants.

> The Vaughans are also adventurous and by no means bound to tradition.

The drive leading away from the house starts here and planting alongside it provides sufficient shelter for luxuriant specimens of the Australian and Tasmanian tree fern, *Dicksonia antarctica*.

Crech ar Pape has been made by expert hands and, even more important perhaps, looked after and continuously adjusted by the same couple. They are sharp-eyed and self-critical and have the highest standards in design and cultivation. These may seem obviously necessary ingredients for the best sort of gardening but they are rarely found. The Vaughans are also adventurous and by no means bound to tradition. This explains why the three of us who twice visited the same not too easily reached spot in two years were so utterly absorbed by what we saw, and impressed by the fertility and freshness of the ideas that had been poured into it.

A pale yellow hemerocallis (right), in sharp contrast to the pink domes of a green-leaved smoke bush – Cotinus coggygria – in flower. Later this will become a pinkish haze, gradually changing to grey, which earns it the alternative name of wig bush.

The round garden at Crech ar Pape (below) has a strong design, softened by plants. The paving throughout is of granite sets, once used in the old roads but superseded by tarmac.

Different varieties of blue agapanthus are generously repeated throughout the garden. They are at their most splendid in July (left).

Timothy Vaughan is a keen plantsman but knows that the flimsier kinds, like Coreopsis verticillata *'Moonbeam', here seen contrasting in shape with spires of* Kniphofia *'Little Maid', must be planted in bold groups (below).*

The lower garden (preceding pages) is on a steep slope leading down to a sunken area where Hakonechloa macra *'Aureola', a golden-variegated grass, replaces the water that you might have expected. Clipped evergreens give fibre to the whole garden, pulling the softer plantings together.*

Hedging, in this part (below) of bay laurel, Laurus nobilis, *is vital for privacy, shelter and a solid background. The much-planted* Hakonechloa macra *(which is taller than 'Aureola') has an important role in its repetition but also moves gracefully in the wind.*

Granite sets, laid in squares to form a diamond pattern, lead the eye down this vista to a central planting of blue and white agapanthus. With the mown grass being at a higher level than the granite, another dimension is brought in. The grasses are a different texture from the firmer shrubs.

This large, glazed pot, surrounded by box, makes a comfortable feature at the divide of two central vistas. All the paths are generous in width, allowing room for plants from adjacent borders to overlap and also a certain amount of self-seeding by low-growing plants.

Colours, shapes and textures create their own sense of harmony. The large, grey globe is formed by the New Zealand Leptospermum lanigerum. *In front of it is the contrast of upright stems from a self-supporting ivy,* Hedera helix *'Conglomerata'.*

Symphonic
Movements

by Mirabel Osler

The advantage of doubling the number of table and chairs by reflecting them in a large sheet of mirror means I appear more hospitable than I am (left). I did take care to tilt the glass forward (facing north) to avoid seeing myself – which was not my motive – and to keep it low enough to avoid deceiving the birds.

*T*HERE IS SOMETHING fundamental to owning

a garden that leaches into every aspect of living. In whatever country, whatever size – acres or a back yard – a garden spills into our lives, continually filling and receding with a magnetism that is impossible to ignore. Our gardens are not merely beautiful places possessed as a single entity, such as a house, horse, diamond or motor car which can be used, admired, ignored or deliberately paraded. Once established, they make continual demands on us. We carry them as an ideal image, forever tugging at our imaginations with their volatile potential. And yet. Only dogs are as forgiving as gardens.

MIRABEL OSLER

Provocative as well as humorous, Mirabel Osler writes at the other end of gardening books – not 'how to' but of the spirit. Her books *A Gentle Plea for Chaos, A Breath from Elsewhere, In the Eye of the Garden* and *The Secret Gardens of France* are idiosyncratic and personal. ♣

I find that forgiveness happens in my own garden year after year, whether in spring or autumn. At times, when I want to write, I treat my 70 × 30-foot area abominably by turning my back on those pleas for attention beyond the window. In spite of such negligence, the plants and trees respond immediately to cherishing, however tardy it is in coming. Spring bulbs appear, though planted just before Christmas; an autumn clear-up postponed until March never seems to hold back the peonies from blooming or the roses from flourishing.

Say the word 'garden' and I think particularly of those that have had lasting resonance, where ideas are absorbed, some to be drawn into my own urban setting. The late Nancy Lancaster's garden at Haseley Court, Oxfordshire, is one. Although she came from Virginia, hers was my ideal English garden with its formality in parts, its secrecy in others, its stylish use of colour on arches, chairs, trellis and pergolas, and the consummate skill with which she incorporated ideas brought back from Italy and elsewhere. Never repetitive, her garden had movements as in a symphony.

Another is Chilcombe, set in sweeping Dorset countryside, the garden belonging to Caryl and John Hubbard. Almost led by the nose, you move through specific areas defined by espaliered fruit trees or rose arbours. Everything is so generously seductive, with numerous seats for each change of light, that were I forced to fritter away my whole summer among its comforting intimacy I would willingly consent.

High above the city of Lyon – the murmur of traffic far below like the undertow of a distant ocean – you enter a rosy paradise.

A garden with a totally different temperament is Odile Masquelier's rose garden in France where her *affaire des roses* brought her worldwide fame and the presidency of the International Conference on Old Roses. High above the city of Lyon – the murmur of traffic far below like the undertow of a distant ocean – you enter a rosy paradise. A novice gardener, wondering whether to plant a rose or not, should visit La Bonne Maison. They would be in no doubt when they left. But look out. Odile has such a voracious appetite for these shrubs that anyone longing for grasses and decking should not bother to board the TGV. Molly Chappellet's Vineyard Garden on Pritchard Hill in California is a completely different place. One that is at variance with the above three – four if I include my own. This garden haunts me. Ever since I first saw it, I hold the garden in my mind's eye as a place of such perfection it's hard not to compare it with those in other countries. But that's not fair. Where else – well certainly not in England – is there this same sense of space and clarity of light that suffuses the golden arc of the Napa Valley in northern California? Obviously the effect varies according to season, but when I was there in May light and irises (two elements that are sublimely complimentary) transfixed me to the spot. Since then, my intention has been to return one autumn to see the crimson leaves of the vines, the changing brilliance of foliage, sunflowers, maize and slanting sunlight. Unfortunately like so many of my other intentions these have been stillborn.

Ideally when visiting a garden I would choose to free-fall: devoid of preconceptions, unaccompanied by the owner, undistracted by dialogue and certainly by anything that came between me and my own antennae. That would be my ideal. But it's seldom achieved. However, if it were, then not until later would come the leading question. '*Who* on earth is the person who's created this place. We must talk.'

Look, I know I haven't seen a great number of gardens. I haven't even been to Australia, Holland or South Carolina, so my garden-yardstick is pathetic. And although I have seen pictures of these places and I long to go, if I never managed to travel any more, Molly's garden would satiate a great number of unfulfilled regrets.

You can never see Venice for the *first time* twice.

So it is with Molly's garden. There is no going back. At least not back to the first time I crossed the threshold and held my breath in astonishment on finding a garden that integrates into the landscape with such delicacy the word 'design' would be a crass intrusion. That first sighting is etched forever as a tattoo in my memory. Any second visit inevitably carries its own partiality.

So what makes her garden so special? My first answer would be that here is a gardener who, owning a spectacular site, has used such an unaccented touch everything she has planted appears to have evolved as

naturally as the ancient outcrops of volcanic rock that rise like humpback whales from the billowing land. Only a gardener of sensitivity could have avoided overstating the obvious.

Until I came to the Vineyard Garden I'd always thought that had I the chance of dealing with a view – I don't mean a pretty scene of cows grazing in a distant pasture but a really wide horizon – I should start by hiding it. This conviction had come about years ago from seeing, within stone-walled court-yards of hilltop monasteries in Greece, unexpected glimpses through an *oeil-de-boeuf*, framed classical landscapes of cypress and olive trees. Those glimpses convinced me that a view should be hidden. Walls, hedges or trees – anything solid and obstructive – would be constructed to stop the horizon from top-pling into the garden before I deliberately created drama by contriving panoramic vistas bold enough to leave one gasping. Yet here – in Molly's gar-den 1,700 feet above the Napa Valley – she has made no attempt to tame the view. Rather she flaunts it. Everything is on show. Her garden has no end. She has allowed it to move seamlessly into the valley and beyond; into the distance, into the rising wooded skyline to where further hills, smudged by shadowy wilderness, vanish into the vastness of America.

Before I went to California I already knew of the famed Merlots, Cabernets, Chardonnays of the region but, because I had visions of the intensive wine-growing country in France, my first sight of the Napa Valley was a revelation. Mountains, hills, oak woods, knolls, spinneys and copses broke up the terrain. Bosky hollows appeared arbitrarily in the middle ground; clouds were reflected in a lake in the valley bottom, and the formless verdancy surrounding the orderly rows of Chappellet vines was nothing like the regimented acres of Burgundy or Alsace. The Napa countryside is so fragmented by bulks of greenery that instead of viewing production on a repetitive scale, here was a setting for some pastoral opera of gargantuan dimensions or a performance of *A Midsummer Night's Dream* with a cast of colossi.

> Gardeners who shun disorder – who risk forfeiting unforeseen dimensions by obsessive control – would find here a beguiling alternative.

Molly is a boulder devotee. At first she and her husband Donn tried subjugating their landscape with strategically placed dynamite, but when their inherited monoliths proved to be unassailable by manmade strategy, Molly acquiesced and worked with, not against, the Pritchard Hill landscape. Rather than warfare, she used plants to complement the form and texture of the boulders, which she came to honour for having been *in situ* for thousands of years.

Stone is the predominant component of the garden, lying on or just below the surface in profusion, and providing a natural material most of us would die for. Built as low retaining walls, the stones were used to form terraces such as you see in olive groves in countries of the Mediterranean. Seen from above, these walls delineate the natural movement of the land as you look down on swathes of colours muted enough not to eclipse the distance. Whereas from below, as you walk along paths covered with bark like deep layers of grated chocolate, you brush against bordering tufts of nepeta blurring the terraces' stone edges, or you peer into the hearts of overhanging roses where their fragrance is almost at nose-level. Look up – there against the sky are the translucent petals of hundreds of irises flourishing among stones. They flank the contours of the falling land with their mauve, ecru, blue and yellow petals in fragile contrast to their blades of rigid leaves.

Being a total gardener with neither tunnel vision nor a compulsive urge for supremacy over wayward behaviour, Molly allows rose petals to lie where they fall. Autumn leaves lie where they drop, drooping boughs overhang paths forcing passers-by to bend their heads. Gardeners who shun disorder – who risk forfeiting unforeseen dimensions by obsessive control – would find here a beguiling alternative. A peerless lily is peerless, yes, but that's only part of it. Uniformity may be restful in its way but of equal merit are the inconsequential attributes, the things that happen naturally or by sheer chance from wind, feral flowers, or the angle of shadows. These natural forces create a garden's atmosphere just as much as the owner's expertise.

Foreign as this garden appeared at first – and I had never seen anything like it – there are many familiar plants. Humble things we love and grow in profusion at home. Patches of penstemon (those great survivors with their wide palette of colours); dollops of blue borage and forget-me-nots; aromatic artemisia with silver-grey foliage; buddleias, lavender and tree mallows. Nowhere is there a single flowerbed – not in the English sense at least. Instead cistus, valerian, euphorbia, sage and santolina thrive in the shallow soil between boulders where a clutter of tulips grow in their shade. Pritchard Hill is not a place of exotica; it's a superb landscape enhanced by form, colour and without a lawn in sight. There had not been any attempt to make even a single patch of striped lawn anywhere. (No wonder the place seemed alien.) Whereas we think a lawn is essential for young children, Molly's six – all grown up now – had trees to climb, hidden thickets to nest in, innumerable seats and hidden trysting corners, as well as the freedom to ride their ponies between rows of vines.

Plants with immediate impact are the cardoons. Glaucous and dominant, with sharply incised leaves, they rise majestically from among fluffier things at their base. Equally impressive are the self-seeded artichokes with their eight-foot stately stance, sculptured heads and leaves with veins on the back as defined as those on the hands of an aged workman. Later in the year Molly brings indoors great stems of cardoons and artichokes with their petrified heads, crackly and silvery, to fill an empty log basket, a corner of a guest room, or some discarded four-gallon container that once had a practical use but now serves as a decorative receptacle. She might place a single decapitated cardoon flower among books on a shelf or hang a few head-down from a hook

in the kitchen. Her flower, vegetable and bough arrangements are as much a part of Molly's garden as the bulbs, roses and clematis growing outside. While she is pruning a shrub or tree, she has already transported the amputated limbs indoors, imagining where best to place them and in what. Fallen fruit is gleaned for the house; heaps of orange or tawny-textured husks lie in piles under a pendulous bough of a pruned shrub standing in a bucket; fir cones, coils of bark, pine needles or snails' shells are decorative bounty Molly uses among persimmons spread across a chest.

There are no defining boundaries between indoors and outdoors. Quite simply the garden flows in and out of the house. Lunching at the Vineyard Garden, the long table laid with a pink tablecloth under the trees may have among the napery and china a miscellaneous collection of flowers gathered early that morning or maybe bundles of vine prunings lying like spillikins beside the wine bottles.

Views and rocks are intrinsic to the garden. But so are trees. As a visitor you aren't led into deliberately moving from one part of the garden to the next by the influence of its design; instead you drift. Imperceptibly you find your gaze turning to the varieties of mimosa, mulberry, ailanthus, the *Magnolia grandiflora* and the magnificent sixty-foot maple, *Acer macrophyllum*, planted by a bird. Other trees around the house are liquidambar, crab apple, flowering cherry, the aromatic camphor tree, *Cinnamomum camphora* – too tender for Britain – and a five-hundred-year-old oak, *Quercus agrifolia*. Among the Pritchard Hill woods are oaks, horse chestnuts, dogwoods and ornamental varieties of the strawberry tree (*Arbutus unedo*). What are so special to our eyes are the noble *madroños* of California (*Arbutus menziesii*) that can grow to a hundred feet. The trees have dark oval leaves with bluish-white undersides; flowers that are whitish panicles; small orange fruit and bark that sheds mahogany coils. Among the shrubs are tall evergreen manzanita (*Arctostaphylos manzanita*) with bark as shiny as a well-used saddle and pinkish flowers that in early spring smother the sea-green leaves.

In the wilder areas are meadows of dwarf lupins, daisies, mallows, poppies and others that would undoubtedly bring cheer to Miriam Rothschild's heart with her controlled disorder in Northamptonshire where she fosters butterflies. In Molly's unregimented kitchen garden peppers, pumpkins, squashes, kohlrabi and kale appear like an Impressionist painting when seen through the feathery fronds of bronze fennel. Shadows among the distant woods are the same deep purple hue of the cabbages and salvias, aubergines (eggplants to Molly) and onions.

...an interlude, a place to escape to through the kitchen.

When writing about Pritchard Hill it's impossible to ignore a major element to the property: the Chappellet winery. The metamorphosis that Molly and Donn had undertaken in the late 1960s, from an urban life in Los Angeles to Pritchard Hill, must have been as transforming as a dragonfly unfurling its wings or more prosaically the simple act of filling their lungs with unpolluted air. From their first year's vintage the Chappellet wine acquired a great reputation. The two components of wine and flowers are integrated in a way that is in contrast to many other places where the frontier between commerce and sensuality are deliberately defined. Farmers who have a garden, for instance, want the world of manure kept separate from bees scrounging among the foxgloves. An art collector I knew in France used his garden as a sanctuary of bedding plants in contrast to his collection of paintings hanging on walls covered by black velvet.

Here it is different. To find a garden that is bonded to a working production – in this case viticulture – has an irresistible attraction. I love the Chappellet collaboration. I envy those who can do it. There is something whole and satisfying in seeing the physical unity of bits of someone's life coming together in this way. My own town garden is merely an interlude, a place to escape to through the kitchen. The Vineyard Garden is a way of life.

The symbiosis between static and non-static is exemplified in Molly's informal planting (left). Everything she has planted appears to have evolved as naturally as the ancient outcrops of volcanic rock.

Foliage as soft as underwater seaweed in contrast to sculptured leaves (below) is a cardinal element in the Vineyard Garden.

Irises and arum lilies flank the contours of the falling land (overleaf). How I envy Molly a landscape where clouds and water are forever shifting the perspective, and where floral profligacy in the foreground flows seamlessly into the vastness of America.

A suffusion of mild colours and the unrestrained density of plants exactly prove the genius of knowing when to loosen gardening control. Borage, California poppies and valerian, in swathes of pinks and white, flow among the boulders at the feet of roses and hibiscus.

Lamb's lugs and fennel (right). Soft against soft; downy against filaments; grey against green – whatever makes it – contrasts of texture and degrees of greenness are essential to gardens.

Irises grow among Molly's boulders as naturally as bindweed infests my garden, only, here, trespass is a virtue. In the right terrain their wanton vagrancy can be a bonus. Because a camera censors overall vision, we see what the photographer chooses for us to see: subtlety of colours. Through Vivian's narrowing lens we pause among muted sulphur and brimstone, transparency and pallor.

In May, sunlight and mist. Come later in the year to discover how the mood changes when leaves of irises spike the air with rigid conformity.

An Inner World

by ANNA PAVORD

Under the heavy, spreading boughs of a medlar (left), the central path of my kitchen garden leads through a rough hazel arch to a sunny south wall beyond. In summer the arch is smothered with old-fashioned sweet peas and purple-podded beans. On the stone wall are fan-trained apricots, peaches, greengages and pears.

'**T**HE FIRST PURPOSE of a garden is to be a place of quiet beauty such as will give delight to the eye and repose and refreshment to the mind,' said the plantswoman Gertrude Jekyll in *A Gardener's Testament*, written towards the end of her life. In the torrents of words that are written about design and colour and plantsmanship, we sometimes forget that a garden must feed our soul as well as our eyes. There is a link between the two, of course, but in fussing about the exact shade of blue for the delphiniums, the line of a path, the placing of a terracotta pot, we become obsessed with incident. The garden fractures

ANNA PAVORD

Well known to television audiences and Radio 4 listeners, Anna Pavord is a highly acclaimed writer as well as a broadcaster. The Tulip, *to which she devoted years of research, is written with all the passion and verve of a detective story. She is gardening correspondent for the* Independent, *associate editor of* Gardens Illustrated *and the author of widely praised gardening books including* The New Kitchen Garden *and* The Border Book. *The figurehead was a wedding present in the days when home was a vast wooden sailing barge.* ♣

into a series of 'features'. Repose and refreshment fly out over the cunningly distressed garden fence.

The gardens I most value are those where you feel, quite palpably, that you are stepping over the threshold into a different world, one that has nothing to do with anger, frustration or sorrow. As a Hindu leaves his shoes at the entrance to the temple, you temporarily cast off life's grubbier aspects and float. Tranquillity. That is why I so love Mapperton, near Beaminster in Dorset. It is not a showy place. The planting is leafy and comfortable. It does not have the huge blazing herbaceous borders considered *de rigueur* in posh country gardens. But sitting on the edge of the great lawn to the north of the stone house, gazing over the valley below, I want the world to stop, there and then.

Mapperton reveals its delights slowly and elegantly. The drive, lined with tall lime trees, leads you down to a group of honey-coloured Ham stone buildings. 'There can hardly be anywhere a more enchanting manorial group,' commented the architectural historian Nikolaus Pevsner. On the left is the house, with chimney stacks like twists of barley sugar and heraldic beasts crouched on the gable ends. Most of it was built in the sixteenth and seventeenth centuries and it makes an 'L' shape, turned into a 'U' by the church of All Saints that adjoins it on the right. On the other side of the entrance drive, two almost matching stable blocks continue the arms of the 'U', facing each

other across a little green, planted with a walnut tree. Swallows swoop about the forecourt, flighting over the roofs like tiny jets. The air is full of their twittering.

Even before I've set foot in the garden I feel good. Partly this has to do with the beauty of the buildings themselves, made when west Dorset was rich with wool and flax. Then the riches disappeared, leaving Mapperton behind. It sits, rooted in its own microcosm, oblivious to fashion, marking time with a clock that ticks to a very slow beat. And it is quiet, so quiet that the crowing of the bantam cockerel scuffing around in the yard echoes through the valley like a clarion. The garden waits, hidden to the north and east of the house, the way in through stone gate piers crowned by lead eagles.

The entrance court is tiny, dominated by paired drums of clipped bay, set either side of the path leading to the front door. A huge *Magnolia delavayi* with paddle-shaped leaves looms out from the house wall, next to a path which leads off to the left, round the side of the house, and brings you out to a massive flat lawn. On two sides of the lawn are tall walls swathed in wisteria, bull bay, garrya, honeysuckle, purple-flowered solanum, scented trachelospermum, cercis and ceanothus. In the far corner a stone summerhouse, rather Edwardian in style, is the first sign that anything much has happened at Mapperton since Richard Brodrepp, a county magistrate, smartened up the north front with classical eighteenth-century architraves and sash windows. The summerhouse is the kind of thing that Edwin Lutyens's contemporary, the garden designer Harold Peto, might have introduced to give a hint of a

grand surprise to come. It speaks of leisure. And of pleasure.

The lawn, with its walls on the north and the west sides, is completely enclosed by the house to the south and a new yew hedge to the east. Drawn to explore the summerhouse, you find a stone path that suddenly plunges steeply off the plateau of the lawn and drops you into a completely different world. On the lawn, at the same level as the cattle and sheep grazing in the rough pasture that rises steeply on the other side of the valley, you may have supposed that the entrance court and the lawn are all there is of the garden at Mapperton. But down below, clasped between the steep shoulders of a little valley, you discover a superb formal arrangement of terraces and yew topiary made in the 1920s, by Ethel Labouchere, who came to Mapperton just after the First World War. It is the best garden conjuring trick that I know and one that would be impossible without the peculiarities of this particular piece of land – the house poised above on its platform, the land dropping steeply and suddenly away from it, then rising equally steeply on the far side of the valley.

The centrepiece of this part of the garden is a raised pool, supported on scrolls of acanthus and sprinkled with the pink and white daisy flowers of *Erigeron karvinskianus.* Either side of the pool, steps rise up to small summerhouses, set like hermits' caves into retaining walls. They are thoughtfully provided with fireplaces and I like to think of Mrs Labouchere sitting here on

...at the same level as the cattle and sheep grazing in the rough pasture that rises steeply on the other side of the valley...

a frosty, sunny October morning, looking out over her Italianate garden while sipping hot chocolate beside a warm wood fire. A few tattered remnants of curtain hang from a pole over the entrance. From these dark little caverns either side of the garden, you peer down between balustrades of yew to the pool, plain and dignified. At the top of this enclosed garden, next to the path that brought you down to the valley, is a Ham stone orangery, put up in the late 1950s by Victor Montagu, father of Mapperton's present owner, the Earl of Sandwich. At the bottom is a Petoesque double pergola with thickly clothed stone pillars and wooden roofbeams. Wisteria, *Vitis coignetiae* and clematis fill the air with mad curls. Pergola and orangery are linked by wide, generous steps that drop gradually to the pool, then rise again the other side. Topiary blocks of yew and box march with you along the way.

At the end of the pergola is another retaining wall. The land falls away steeply again to a different part of the garden. A tall square tower, with a tiny wood-panelled room inside, marks the boundary between the two sections. From the cobwebbed window, you look down on a long seventeenth-century canal garden, with clipped cones of yew along the sides. The water is divided into two stretches, the first at a slightly higher level than the second. Between them are sofas of yew, curving round stone seats and a raised dais, frothing with alchemilla. At the end of the canal garden, spiky yuccas and a pair of tall Irish yews mark the finish of the formal layout.

But already, you are aware of a wilder type of garden that begins on the bank, closing in the left-hand side of the canal garden. Tall pines tower over camellias, azaleas, cotinus, cherries and cornus. Below the canal garden, this wild garden, in a totally different mood, continues on down the valley. Gravel paths give way to grass. It is shady and cool. A huge tulip tree, a grove of bamboo, a dawn redwood (*Metasequoia glyptostroboides*), a vast *Magnolia campbellii* and forests of gunnera follow the stream down the valley. This collection of rare shrubs and trees, a kind of '*Hillier's Manual* garden', completely separate from the formal layouts that precede it, was planted by Victor Montagu in the 1960s. Under the trees the grass gets longer, reaching out to the farmland beyond. But even here, where formal walls no longer contain the garden, Mapperton is enclosed within its own world. There are no long views. Above, the house hangs as though at the edge of a cliff. Beyond, at the very end of the garden, there is a bulge of woodland, a high escarpment of pasture. Then sky.

At Mapperton, I am in heaven. But what bearing does the place have on our own garden? On the face of it, very little. Mapperton's advantages – of architecture, of age, of setting – are gifts rarely given to gardeners. And only a millionaire could afford now to lay out a formal garden as splendid as Mrs Labouchere's. Though plants are still cheap, materials and labour are not and a bronze plaque by the pool records that ten people laboured to bring this place into being. Our rectory garden is far smaller and more domestic in scale than Mapperton's manorial acres and we do not have water to play with. We have views though. Almost the best thing about the garden is the prospect from our top lawn, the valley dropping and then rising to a patchwork of fields several miles away. Sometimes they are bright green with new grass. Sometimes they are blue with flax, or cream with the heads of ripening corn. In the long shadows of a September evening, the humps and bumps of long-buried Roman villas rise out of the fields like ghosts.

But even here, where formal walls no longer contain the garden, Mapperton is enclosed within its own world.

What Mapperton showed me was the importance of mood in a garden. And that spaces (voids) are as important as incidents. In a period when garden designers seemed to be obsessed with swoops and whirls, interlocking circles and wavy edges, it reassured me that there was nothing wrong with straight lines. Mapperton taught me to respect texture in a garden: stone, bark, moss, lichen, the matt absorbent green of yew against the shinier, reflecting surface of box. It filled me with regard for the spirit of place that imbues many old gardens and reminded me how important it was to release, enhance that spirit, rather than impose upon it. Mapperton is lushly planted, with overflowingly generous tubs and urns, luxuriant climbers, plants that have been thoughtfully placed. Ominously powerful daturas are massed by the orangery; beautiful plectranthus spill around you in grey waterfalls. But it is not a plantsman's garden. That does not in any way detract from its appeal; rather the reverse. Amassing plants is not the same as making a garden. The whole needs to be a greater construct than the sum of its parts.

When we first came to our house (now twenty-six years ago), we moved very slowly through our garden, which had been neglected for decades. Mostly, it was a matter of releasing its structure, rather than inflicting new lines and directions. Decisions often seemed inevitable, given the lie of the

> ...we planted the medlar tree which my mother brought us. It was almost the first thing we put in.

land and the play of light against shade. Sometimes, when we hacked through wilderness, thinking to make a path, we would discover the stones or scalloped edgings of a much earlier path silted up there, under the leaves, the brambles and nettles. So it was more like archaeology than building and we were always comforted by the notion that our decisions had been made for us, long ago. Most of the early work was concentrated in the old walled kitchen garden, still dissected, we found, into the nine squares of a noughts and crosses grid: two parallel paths running north to south, bisected by another two paths running east to west, the typical lay-out of a seventeenth-century kitchen garden.

Here, we planted the medlar tree which my mother brought us. It was almost the first thing we put in. As soon as the south-facing wall at the bottom was cleared, I planted greengages and peaches, pears and apricots and began the long, slow process of teaching myself how to prune them into espaliers and fans. Why? I don't know. But when you first start to garden, there are so many different aspects that can intrigue you. Some people take to alpines, others to cactus. Some want only to grow monster onions. Others collect rhododendrons or specialize in compost heaps. I'm mad on fruit, particularly pears. You can keep your apples: cold-fleshed, self-satisfied fruit. I'm for pears, melting pears, with skins speckled and freckled with russet spots and flesh that dissolves like butter in your mouth. 'Beurre Hardy', a French pear, raised about 1820, has always kept a special place in my affections because it was the first pear I ever planted. It produces a big, chunky fruit, handsome, well-conformed with a shiny yellowish-green skin thickly overlaid with russet. The flesh is white with the faintest hint of pink, melting, juicy, completely without the graininess that ruins some good-looking pears. Hovering around it when you bite into it is a muted whiff of rose water. It is a Château Lafitte of pears.

Pruning fruit trees is not a subject you can pick up from a book. The picture on the page never looks like anything you have got in front of you in the garden. Trial and error (a lot of error in the beginning) taught me a lot. So did men such as Ron Nettle, dead now, but for many years head gardener at Rotherfield Park in Hampshire. The heart of his empire was the great walled kitchen garden where he had his glasshouses and where he grew some of the best trained fruit trees in the country. Against the red brick outside, his espalier pears sat neat as tramlines. In the glasshouses, apricots had been painstakingly trained for years to make fans that stretched the whole length of the centre passage. He reckoned to pick at least sixty pounds of fruit from each tree. He didn't fuss around with camel hair brushes or rabbit's tails to pollinate the flowers. He just tapped the branches from time to time to shake out the pollen. Temperature was the key, he said. If the fruit was to set, nothing less than 60°F would do.

He had little time for what he called 'college-trained' men. 'You can pass any damned exam on this earth and still not be able to grow a decent pear,' he used to say, daring you to disagree. Pears, I learned from him, are easier to train than apples, more pliable. But for the best results, they've got to be against a wall. Mr Nettle favoured west walls. They held the warmth longer in the evening. Against ants and wasps, he waged implacable war. To protect his pears, he used wasp bags made of tiffany, like lace curtain material, only stiffer. Each had a drawstring cord and, before the wasps were active, he slipped each fruit on the trees into a bag and pulled the string tight. He didn't consider that a labour, because once he'd got the fruit in the bag, he was sure of it.

Will I ever have the patience to use tiffany bags? Sadly, I don't think I will. But often Mr Nettle's shade hovers over me, truculent, demanding, perfectionist, when I am in our own kitchen garden, tying in the Morello cherry fanned out on a north wall, or pruning the 'Jargonelle' pear. 'If a job is worth doing, it's worth doing properly.' He'll never let me forget that maxim at least. And I'm always happier among the fruit and vegetables than I am anywhere else in the garden. I've always loved kitchen gardens: the order, the productivity, the pre-ordained cycle of sowing and cropping. That is one thing Mapperton cannot provide – a proper old-fashioned kitchen garden with vine houses and peach houses, box-edged borders and fruit trees fanned immaculately against the walls. But in high summer in my own garden, when passion flowers drip luxuriantly out of the pergola and roses fling their arms wildly across the paths, the kitchen garden is where you will most likely find me, wallowing in cabbages.

A narrow flowerbed (above) borders the walk that runs underneath the high retaining wall between the garden and the steep pasture on the far side. Looking south (top), the view falls away into the wild valley; the orangery acts as a backstop at the north end.

A complex double pergola (right) closes off the end of the top part of the garden, before a steep fall to the next level. Vines, clematis and old-fashioned roses clothe the pillars.

Exuberant and informal plantings explode between the strictly formal clipped pieces of topiary in the Mapperton garden (overleaf). As in all the best gardens, a clever balance is kept between the two opposing elements. The orangery provides shelter for semi-tender exotics.

Below the pergola (seen on pages 184–5) lies the elegant mirror of the canal garden, split into two halves, one slightly higher than the other. Two curving hedges of yew provide the backs to stone seats set between the two stretches of water.

A well-planted woodland walk runs along the east side of the canal garden, giving occasional glimpses of the formal clipped yew cones that march either side of the water. Maples, hamamelis and cherry give the area a faintly Japanese air.

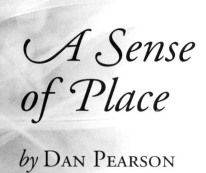

A Sense of Place

by Dan Pearson

My garden in London could never be big enough but I have tried to plant it as freely as possible. Amongst more static plantings, there are groups of informal perennials that chart not only the passing of the seasons but also the elements that influence the garden. Here (left), the mobile Stipa barbata *is an airy contrast to jagged* Eryngium giganteum. *Further into the planting (seen in the photograph on page 194),* Eryngium agavifolium *introduces architecture amongst the informality of* Digitalis ferrruginea, salvia *and* Verbena bonariensis.

SOMEONE SAID TO

me once that if you could find and recreate what you were lost in as a child, this was the way to a level of contentment as an adult. I found this peaceful place at the age of five or six when I discovered the alchemy of gardening and I am convinced that, if I live to be a hundred, the world of garden making will continue to offer fulfilment.

Gardens are, after all, places that ask you to look again. In my mind I often return to the ones I inhabited as a child, all of which had their own very particular identity. They were some of my greatest inspirations and, to a degree, I still

DAN PEARSON

One of Britain's most influential and innovative designers, Dan Pearson has been creating gardens and winning prizes, including Chelsea Gold, since 1984. He trained at Wisley and Kew and was awarded travelling scholarships to Spain, India and Israel. His television career began with a film about his roof garden for Gardeners' World. *He is a columnist for the* Sunday Times, *the author and presenter of* The Garden, *about the making of Home Farm, and, with Terence Conran, the author of the highly acclaimed* The Essential Garden Book.

draw upon their essence in my work as a garden maker. I have various people to thank for realizing that the garden was a good place for me to be that early on and that it was quite all right to allow me to be there, apparently, on my own. My parents allowed me room to indulge my interest in patches around their garden. My father grew the flowers, the seven-foot 'lavatory lily' planted beside the outside toilet being the best *Lilium auratum* I can remember seeing. My mother grew the vegetables. I never felt that I was excluding myself from the world – to the contrary, the time spent alone gazing into the pond at the end of the garden or nurturing my seedlings was an engagement with life in a world that never ceases to surprise.

Geraldine Noyes who lived up the road was my first gardening soulmate. Retired but never old, she would return from trips to the mountains of Europe with plants, wrapped tight in moist tissue paper, secreted in the boot of her Morris Minor. She would squeeze these 'exotic' plants with their equally exotic stories of collection into the spillage of her garden. Amongst drifts of wild poppies, anchusa, scarlet pimpernel and seeding grasses, there were beds of bearded iris and eschscholzia. She had a small pond bulging with water-lilies and home to red dragonflies, a rockery with ramondas and *Fritillaria pyrenaica* (smuggled), an orchard full of cowslips and idiosyncratic shrub roses and a vast *Magnolia grandiflora* that clattered up by the house. There were always treasures amongst the weeds and the weeds were never an issue to her.

On each and every day of the year, she had and still has a posy of something picked from the garden on the kitchen table.

When I was ten we moved along the road to a semi-derelict house behind a vast overgrown laurel hedge. All you could see from the lane was a solitary birch tree growing from the chimney but, descending through a gap in the hedge, you plummeted into the shade and chaos of an acre garden that had fallen into decay. It had been planted in the early nineteen hundreds by Miss Joy, the spinster who lived there until she became overwhelmed by it all. The garden pressed itself against the glass of the mouldering windows so that a strange aquatic light filled the rooms inside. Akebia vine had found its way under the skirting boards and was trailing around the furniture. The rootstock of a rambling rose had overtaken a rotting balcony and the only way down to the old orchard was a tiny track that Miss Joy had kept clear to stoke the fire that heated the crumbling lean-to in which there was a failing camellia.

Nettles towered overhead and bamboo and brambles colonized the remains of an old lawn. A vast turkey oak that Miss Joy had planted from a seed brought back from her travels formed a perfect dome in the centre of the garden and here in its dense shade was the only respite from the undergrowth.

As we cleared the old trees we found a wintersweet and clerodendrums, a fetid pond clogged with leaves and, one day, as we cut back a huge branch of laurel, a pair of long borders. The garden came back to life as new light spilled in. The old orchard was transformed for three weeks in the spring with a carpet of bluebells and primroses that must have crossed with polyanthus in the past to produce every shade from grey to plum. The vast rhododendrons also began to bloom again, slashing the woodland with colour. But in clearing the undergrowth to make sense of the garden, one tree leaning on the next would fall quietly in the night. Without knowing it, we had disturbed the balance.

I took over one of the long borders, my father the other, and as we gardened in this place it became clear that it was pointless fighting the shade and the sense of wilderness: this was part of the place, the sense of place. It was altogether wiser and more fulfilling to garden on the side of nature here, despite the frustrations. Silver plants and moisture lovers would have to be enjoyed elsewhere.

It was about this time that I became inspired by the garden of Mrs Frances Pumphrey at Greatham Mill. I went to visit every weekend to see her masterful combinations of plants in this larger-than-life cottage garden. She was not only a masterful gardener, she also had a brilliant eye and every corner of the mill garden was packed to bursting. There was an exuberance and a freedom to the planting and the garden was filled with unusual plants that were used well in combination. *Geranium psilostemon* clambered through *Buddleja globosa* and dark corners were filled with textured shade lovers. It was a plantsman's paradise and Mrs P. was a character. Her response to many tales I had to tell her about my own garden was: 'Well, bugger me!' She was great fun and regaled me with stories of flying through the Himalayas in a two-man plane. She brought the world of plants to life. After a year or so of weekend visits, she asked me if I would like a Saturday job and for the next four years I spent all my earnings on her plant stall, building my long yellow border and experimenting in the other, wilder areas in the garden at home. I was

…wiser
and more fulfilling
to garden on the side
of nature…

gardening on the wild side and with the freedom to experiment that you have only when you are learning.

During my training at Wisley, I soaked up the garden there, looking at plants as individuals, learning about how to grow them and what their relatives were. It was as if each specimen had a magnifying glass trained over it, revealing information to be absorbed before I moved on. This rather blinkered vision lasted for two years, until I was awarded a scholarship to visit the mountains of northern Spain. The trip was a revelation and to a degree it connected straight back to my earlier years of gardening. For the first time I realized that it was nature that had all the answers and this was where plants looked their happiest. I started to see them for the mood they conveyed and for the way in which they lived in association. My travels took me to the Middle East and to the Himalayas to look at plants in the wild and it was in these years that I gained my love of landscape or, to be precise, a fascination with the sense of place and, although I would still rather spend my time in landscape than in a garden, it is gardens which capture a sense of place that work for me.

The arum lilies have run riot along a wet ditch...

A sense of place is a subtle thing and it manifests itself in the most unlikely places. The Green Thumb community gardens in Manhattan, for instance, are a complete joy. They are free expressions of the people who garden them. Utilizing empty lots of land, the gardens are makeshift and transitory but there is a passion here and a vigour which is so much about the city. At the same time they are the antidote to the city. This is gardening with no rules. Runner beans climb up rusted bedsteads, tomatoes and zinnias compete for the sunshine. Totem poles are fashioned from junk and stuffed toys in one lot and juxtaposed with a chinoiserie gazebo in the next. There is a sense of community here, the gardens bringing together people from all walks of life.

In complete contrast, the gardens at Ninfa in southern Italy are another inspiration. They are about a romantic fantasy, the old walls of the ruined village festooned with ancient roses with twisted trunks as thick as your arm. I first visited this garden in late May, just as the light was fading. The heat of the day had agitated the essential oils in a meandering river of lavender and fireflies glinted in the shade over the water that slides through the garden. The water itself is the greatest surprise. Coursing from the hill in a deep clear river, it is elemental. Green-streamered water weeds sway in its current and you can

smell the moisture. It is a complete tonic to the hot dustiness that predominates in the valley. The water has been divided up into ribbons that charge through the garden as guides along paths and as playful eddies in the dark shade. There is one point where one ribbon crosses another and this is pure joy. It makes you want to laugh.

The planting at Ninfa is old and established and there is an air of neglect that is, I suspect, part of its charm. Ferns colonize roofless rooms and decrepit benches are concealed under vine-choked arbours. The arum lilies have run riot along a wet ditch and terracotta campsis scales the walls of the ruined castle. But there is a feeling of balance here. You are not aware of the garden as a design, it is a meander of moods and this is its essential magic.

Design for design's sake is something I have always battled against and my

...the senses are better teased and tickled than commanded to attend.

favourite gardens are those in which you are transported rather than held to attention to look at the designer's creation. Gardens are places that are ultimately sensual and the senses are better teased and tickled than commanded to attend. The fact that gardens can work on such subtle levels is a potential liberation and the magic is that this liberation can be different for each person.

Good design is a celebration of the place and an ingenious use of a space. The Donnell Garden in California by Thomas Church is a good example. Still deeply modern, though fifty years old, it relies on minimal ingredients. Stone, trees, shadow patterns, a view and water. The borrowed view, the celebration of light and the simplicity of line – these are the secret to this garden.

Although I had always found the rigour and aesthetic of the gardens of Japan alienating, I knew the real thing had to be experienced to be understood. I was there for six weeks in total, visiting modern work in Tokyo and the historical gardens in Kyoto. There are too many high points to recount but one experience may convey the approach to their aesthetic. One evening we went to visit the owner of a cherry tree nursery as it was April and cherry blossom season. Outside the nursery on the by-road was a vast, domed weeping cherry. As dusk fell, nursery staff stoked the braziers placed to illuminate and celebrate the tree. We stood under its enormous canopy with many other people who had pulled off the road to witness this spectacle. The flickering cave of blossom was a moment of perfection.

This attention to detail was borne out again and again in Japan: the mud wall in the Zen gravel garden at Ryoan-ji which is an object of such beauty that it has been designated a national treasure; the Noguchi garden in a Tokyo foyer that is no more than stone and water; the trees or rocks with raffia bracelets to single them out; and the single stone in the pathway to bar the way. Even a plate of tempura vegetables became an aesthetic experience. Reaching this level of awareness is taught, it is in the culture and the best gardens use it to enhance the experience of being in that place.

The moss garden of Saiho-ji in Kyoto was one of my favourites. On entering the temple courtyard or anti-chamber, we had to remove our shoes and take part in a ritual chant. As Westerners, we were given ink and paper with a text in Japanese printed delicately over the surface. Over the course of half an hour, we had to trace over this chant with brush and ink whilst the monks chanted in the other half of the room. Only then were we released into the garden and it was clear that we had needed this conditioning to be able to experience the place.

A small stone path switches around the garden, turning from left to right and towards and away from an opaque expanse of still water. In contrast to the horizontal plane of water, there are dark trunks of lofty conifers that allow in shafts and pools of light, shining on seemingly natural camellias and acers, the acers when we were there being at that moment of perfection just after they have come into leaf. Closer observation revealed each tree to be an exercise in control, its limbs subtly thinned to achieve exactly the correct balance.

On the undulating surface of the garden there is nothing but moss, an emerald carpet that cushions and drifts to the base of the trees and to the water's edge. On the moss fallen camellia flowers are left to lie in the right places and in the right quantity to break the control – or to add to it. This interpretation of nature has pared down the ingredients and, in so doing, proves the maxim that less is more. We stood in the apparent silence – the sounds not far away of urban Kyoto filtered by the atmosphere of the place – and felt the light, felt the break in the water as a fish rose to the surface, felt the intensity of green and the movement of the wind in foliage. The garden was a completely sensory experience and each one of us was affected.

I felt privileged later in the trip to meet the designer of one of the simplest and most refined gardens I saw in Japan. Mr Kubo had trained as a landscape painter but wanted to work in three dimensions. He showed me the small garden he had created for a monk at Kengo-In. He had walled out the surrounding suburbs, yet his treatment of the space is clear, minimalist and modern. A hill in the distance, borrowed to become the focus of the view, has been brought into the garden with a series of curvaceous clipped azaleas. Like river-washed boulders, these mounds catch the light and their shapes play with the roundness of the distant hill. Rising from them are artfully pruned cedrus to add a vertical, a further traditional device but tradition with a twist.

From the gravel path twisting between the clipped forms, we stepped up a large stone to reach the wooden veranda. There we sat and talked and soaked in the place, unaware of bustling Kyoto around us but very much in the present.

Ninfa nestles into the land at the base of a series of hot hills. On a well-chosen site, with a river coursing through it, the buildings are all but lost in the profusion of the garden (left).

California poppies seed in the open, sun-filled ruins of the old chapel (overleaf) and mark a contrast to the leafiness of the rest of the garden.

A rustic wooden bridge (below) runs alongside an old Roman bridge over the river. The air here is cool and moist and the plants respond accordingly.

A small grove of bamboo (bottom), which could be out of place here, surrounds a clear spring, but it stands alone as a separate 'event' within the garden.

Gunnera manicata *sit at the edge of the river with their feet in the wet banks (left). They could not be more opulent and are all the better for being massed, adding weight to the ephemeral roses that scale the walls about them.*

The ceilings of some of the old buildings have been reconstructed as vine-covered arbours. An old Vitis coignetiae *covers this one (below, left) and provides welcome shade and enclosure.*

Iris are planted along many of the stream margins in the garden. Though only fleetingly in flower, they light up dark corners and slash the garden with ribbons of colour (below).

Shade and water are vital ingredients at Ninfa and you are never far from either. They are the contrast to the hot dustiness of the land beyond the garden. It is hard to imagine the heat of the sun from the shelter of the shade here (right).

In places, the water has been channelled into fast torrents. This tributary (far right) changes pace where it drops from one level to another and the contrast between the apparently still pool and its cascade are both dynamic and hypnotic in the same instance.

In other parts of the garden, the cascades are more sedate (below) and you will find yourself affected by their pace there also.

Interrelating
Shapes

by DAVID STEVENS

Humour is an indispensable facet of design, and of garden design in particular. We sometimes take ourselves far too seriously, and gravity is the antithesis of a joyful and often capricious landscape. I see this happy chap, with his slightly startled expression (left), every day outside our back door, and he reminds me just how lucky I am.

W HEN STARTING

out on a career we can have little idea how important the very earliest influences are to be, although the threads bound into a lifeline are easy enough to see in retrospect. Fascination with drawing, inspired by living on the wild north Cornish coast, formed the initial strands of my enduring passion for art and landscape. Every free moment was spent in or around the ocean, on long, golden beaches, and scrambling over rocks that were the outliers of high, sculptural cliffs. When weather or darkness drove us inside, I was happy enough copying maps, sketching cartoons and generally

DAVID STEVENS

A leading contemporary garden designer and broadcaster, David Stevens is the winner of eleven Chelsea Flower Show Gold Medals. His prestigious appointments include Professor of Garden Design at Middlesex University, Consultant to the Chelsea America Foundation and Consultant to the Royal National Rose Society. He is the author of many books, including Small Gardens and Backyards, Pergolas and Follies, Town Gardens, Simple Garden Projects, The Outdoor Room, The Garden Book *(with Ursula Buchan),* Gardens by Design, The Garden Design Sourcebook, Garden Walls and Floors *and* Garden Features and Ornament. ❧

messing about with pencils or brushes. Many of my drawings were incredibly detailed explorations of the way shapes relate to one another or fit together and, after a few false starts, it was these that eventually drew me to architecture and then landscape design.

Like many people of my generation, I hadn't a clue as to what to do after leaving school and went through a succession of jobs, ranging from marine underwriting to sales management in a firm producing gold leaf and hot stamping foils. While little of this was to do with design, much of it related to people, which stood me in good stead later on. Gardening mattered little to me in those early days. Then, when I was twenty-four, I met a landscape gardener who, quite by chance, asked me to prepare some sketches for him, and the die was cast. Within a month I had left my safe sales job and was helping to run a garden shop, undertaking rudimentary designs of an appalling standard, driving the delivery van, buying plants, the names of which were a complete mystery, and generally having the time of my life.

My new boss went bust, which was a salutary experience, and I started my own company, laying crazy paving, carrying out garden maintenance and learning the basics of the trade. Pretty quickly, however, the need for design skills became pressing, so I enrolled at Thames Polytechnic to study landscape architecture. The college library was an Aladdin's cave of art and design books. I started to home in on contemporary work, stretching from the Bauhaus to minimalism, which sparked the realization that design is all-encompassing and truly great design brings together art, landscape and much else. Learning alongside students of architecture, we were naturally involved with the built environment, townscape and all kinds of human activity. I discovered Christopher Tunnard's *Gardens in the Modern Landscape*, which at that time was one of the very few books on modernist garden design and innovative urban landscaping. When I picked up a copy of John Brookes' book *Room Outside*, it was a revelation and, having read it endlessly from cover to cover, I was lucky enough to talk my way into a job with John at Syon Park. It was the best thing I could have done!

Working with John Brookes, all these strands began to crystallize when I happened on the awesome achievements of three great pioneers, the buildings of Frank Lloyd Wright and the gardens designed by Sir Edwin Lutyens and Lawrence Halprin.

...the bright light of secret inner courtyards, clothed with bougainvillaea and soothed by the sound of water.

Wright, whose work spans the nineteenth and twentieth centuries, designed buildings that meld with and grow from their immediate surroundings. The thrust of his philosophy was that a building cannot survive in isolation; it must be firmly rooted in the ground. And his organic style was unique, breathtakingly beautiful and revolutionary in its conception, his most audacious works – Fallingwater in Pennsylvania and his Prairie Style houses – both striking and low key in so much that house, garden and landscape blend imperceptibly together. This, too, I realized, is what garden design is about, as our particular medium can surely only be a facet of the others.

Much later, visiting Taliesin West was a near-spiritual landscape experience. From a distance, Wright's winter home and studio for the latter part of his life, lying twenty-six miles north of Phoenix in Arizona, hardly rises above the desert floor, a seemingly inhospitable and barren landscape, dotted with cholla and saguaro cactus, *Carnegiea gigantea* and the occasional ironwood tree (*Ostrya virginiana*). The setting is hauntingly beautiful, but at the same time, hard, brutal and, with mountains in the background, angular. Wright took great pieces of multicoloured basalt rock, mixed with cement, together with sand and gravel from the site, casting them into massive battered walls. He used a combination of 30-, 60- and 90-degree angles in both the floor plan and the elevations, which echo and link with the shapes of the mountains beyond.

Practicality is combined with art as you cross a sculpted ditch to deter rattlers and ascend broad generous steps to pass beneath a pergola of angled trusses. These anchor the drafting room, 'the great workplace', first into the house walls and then the desert floor itself. Roofed in canvas, this room is open to the landscape that flows in to inspire all who work there. As you continue further into the building, turning this way and that, there are spaces with low ceilings and high ceilings, feelings of compression and expansion, continually punctuated by desert views. Eventually you burst out into the bright light of secret inner courtyards, clothed with bougainvillea and soothed by the sound of water.

When Wright built Taliesin West he found ancient Indian petroglyphs, sacred and symbolic carved rocks, which he incorporated within his scheme. It is a measure of the man that these were positioned with the same orientation in which they were found.

Taliesin inspires on many different levels, as art, architecture, landscape and gardens, but does so in a way that underlines their inseparability. It is at once subtle yet complicated, dynamic yet timeless. Not simply a building, the place is an experience and a great, great piece of design.

You would think that a British architect, practising at the turn of the twentieth century would be poles apart from Wright's work of the same period. Edwin Lutyens was the archetypal Englishman, mixing freely with rich clients and bankrupting not a few of them with his beautiful but expensive country houses. But Lutyens was also the most vernacular of designers, having an innate feeling for the siting of a building, the choice of materials and how the whole composition relates to the landscape beyond. He was, possibly, the best garden designer Britain has produced and his work never ceases to be inspiring.

Hestercombe lies on the edge of the Quantock Hills in Somerset, facing south looking over Taunton Deane. Behind the house wooded ground rises sharply, offering protection from cold north winds. We know that Lutyens tried and discarded a number of schemes before settling on the design, clearly working through various permutations. The result, created in 1904–6, is not only gloriously subtle, but also the first opportunity that Lutyens and

Gertrude Jekyll had to develop fully their combined ideas of architecture and gardening.

The main garden, or 'Great Plat' as Lutyens called it, is a perfect square with cross axes of diagonal lawns that cleverly increase the feeling of space. The remaining triangular shapes are given over to planting, subdivided by stone paths that add to the geometric pattern and offer practical access to the beds for maintenance. To east and west of the 'Plat' lie long narrow water gardens and to the north end of each, closest to the house, are positioned pool courts. These are simply exquisite and are viewed through walls that sweep down in flowing curves from either side. Within the intimacy of each court, a circular pool is set in a half-hemisphere that is recessed into the rear wall, a delicate shaft of water dropping into the surface below. Central rills, with devastatingly simple loop pools, run the length of the gardens; planted with aquatics, they add both verticality and perspective to the otherwise perfectly flat plane.

To the south of the 'Plat' a pergola of the old school runs right the way across the garden for over two hundred feet. Nothing about it is flimsy or insubstantial – great stone piers, topped with solid oak beams smothered with climbers. Apart from being a wonderful element in its own right, the pergola in all its strength helps to contain the garden visually, allowing a partial and as a result more tantalizing view of the landscape beyond.

While all of this garden geometry is stunning in its own right, it is Jekyll's planting that brings the whole thing alive, even today since it was beautifully restored in 1973 when almost miraculously her original drawings were found in a potting shed! At the time she was obviously excited to be working with the younger Lutyens and, as well as using dramatic plant combinations at ground level, she planted the great retaining walls with pockets of billowing bloom, softening the overall outline. We tend to forget, nearly a hundred years on, how leading-edge all of this was: the gradation of colour, contrasts of pale flower against dark backgrounds and the bold use of differing plant forms. The effect of the whole composition, gently basking in the summer sun of a hot West Country afternoon, is one that garden designers would do well to emulate in a modern idiom. It also brings home the point that two heads are so often better than one – neither of these great people could have achieved what they did without the other, and we are thankfully the richer for it.

While Wright and Lutyens ploughed their own distinct furrows, it was Lawrence Halprin who really opened my eyes to the Modern Movement in terms of landscape architecture. Halprin represented the second generation of American designers after Thomas Church and Garrett Eckbo, producing a clean and superbly individualistic style that pared away the sentimentality of the old European Beaux-Arts school.

As with any influential individual there is always an element of being the right person at the right time and Halprin, after working in Church's San Francisco office, started his own highly successful practice. His wife Anna, who was a leading *avant-garde* dancer and dance teacher, brought to the partnership a richness born of a quite different artistic medium. The 1950s were a time of enormous expansion on the West Coast, with Halprin and his team working on a fascinating range of urban and domestic projects that allowed them to explore whole new fields of style, theory and practice. No longer, and this was vitally important, were designers imposing their will on the landscape; they were developing their skills through interactive public participation, producing projects that worked for *people*.

Halprin regularly took hiking trips into the High Sierra that runs inland behind the city of San Francisco, to regenerate his creative soul and gain inspiration from the wild terrain. Although he designed a huge number of small gardens, it is his larger-scale work where these stimuli become metamorphosed into built landscape forms, often using sculpturally formed concrete, water and other natural elements, that fascinates me. This ranges from the audacity of the Seattle Freeway Park, which is a wonderland of cascading water, trees and open space, built over an eight-lane highway, to the stark beauty of Ira's Fountain in Portland, Oregon, and Levi's Plaza in San Francisco, which I single out as the design that works for me, on many different levels.

Levi's Plaza is misleading. It is a public park, open to all and used by many, although owned by the company that bears its name, and also a place

...the pergola in all its strength helps to contain the garden visually, allowing a partial and as a result more tantalizing view of the landscape beyond.

of contrasts, movement, forms and symbolism. Everybody, quite rightly, reacts to art in different ways and on a simple level Levi's Plaza is a green space in the bustling heart of a great city where you can unwind alongside a meandering stream. The ground is gently contoured to form the interlocking spurs of a river valley, trees, shrubs and other planting having matured, while you can cross and re-cross the stream by simple stepping stones. For many people this is enough: they can sit, picnic, listen to live music that is regularly staged at lunchtime, and generally enjoy themselves.

Dig a little deeper, however, and a wealth of meaning comes to the surface: this is a journey from mountain to sea, from turbulent upland to lowland tranquillity. Water is life and such a journey is life itself in all its dynamic moods. It is best to start at the source which adjoins the Levi headquarters, a powerful and none too pretty piece of modern architecture. This in itself is a challenge, as the eye and attention needs to be drawn away into the landscape. Moving water is of course the answer and Halprin uses all his ingenuity to create a series of split-level pools, cascades and stepping stones that form a gloriously subtle garden in their own right. The centrepiece to this area is a massive rough-hewn granite block that spews water down its faces into the pool below. This is the visible source that you can easily imagine as a mountain cascade. A few yards away there is a second 'hidden' source, where water wells up from within a smooth concrete cube, as though issuing from some great subterranean spring. Both sources send water skittering and dancing down stairs which are sometimes smooth, sometimes ribbed, but always different, like the landscape that inspired them.

Look at the subtlety of his design, the shapes, the clever innuendoes and, above all, revel in the excitement of the place.

A favourite device of Halprin's, and one that is typically American, is to allow and actively encourage people to involve themselves with his spaces. At Levi's Plaza, as in many of his schemes, the exquisitely detailed stepping stones thread their way across water. Rarely in straight lines, they follow staggered patterns, almost at random, but are delicately placed by a sensitive eye. At times they appear dangerous, passing close to tumbling cascades or seemingly deep pools, and are naturally much loved by children.

Planting is sparse in this 'upland', as of course it would be in the landscape that inspired it. Just a few well-chosen trees and simple blocks of ground cover enhance rather than detract from the underlying purity of the design.

If you visit Levi's Plaza, take your time and *really* look at what is going on here. Halprin is a modern artist, a lover of landscape and above all a social person in that his schemes set out to serve the populace rather than simply seeking self-gratification. Look at the subtlety of his design, the shapes, the clever innuendoes and, above all, revel in the excitement of the place. Walk over the water and alongside the stream into the lowland landscape. Watch people enjoying themselves, listen to the music and, like me, you will come to realize that much good design is unconsciously accepted by all who come in contact with it – that is its purpose and that is its worth.

A garden can rarely exist as a self-contained entity confined within boundaries. By its very nature it must relate to both the house it adjoins and the landscape, town or cityscape that lies beyond. The pots and pillar (left) are a clever device to slow the eye before it drifts out through the low, soft planting to the hazy Somerset countryside.

One of the joys of Hestercombe is the moulding of different levels into a glorious whole. Lutyens' great stone terraces are softened by Jekyll's bold but deft swathes of foliage (below) that cascade, like the breaking surf of my north Cornish childhood, to the levels below.

The rills that form the central axis of the water gardens (overleaf) are an exquisite example of pure yet subtle design. A lesser mortal than Lutyens would never have thought of the delicate loop pools that echo the curving walls and, in turn, enclose the pool courts. All this geometry is counterbalanced by lush borders that in themselves bring enormous power to the composition.

Impeccable detailing is the hallmark of a good garden and a great designer. This classical head (above) spills water into one of the two pool courts at Hestercombe. The patina of age and the self-seeded planting bring maturity to this corner of a remarkable garden, underlining the point that worthwhile design is timeless.

If you have a room with a view, make the most of it! This little window (left) is all the more telling because it compresses the picture in much the same way as a miniature painting. Unexpected visual tricks are the stuff of a great garden, adding their own individualistic subtleties.

Breathing Spaces

by ANNE SWITHINBANK

A large part of my garden is a field-like slope, which used to be grazed or mown. Now, every spring, we watch with excitement as the meadow of grasses and wildflowers rises, rich green at first, studded with colour through early summer, and gradually turning pale and dry before it has its annual cut in August.

$\mathscr{M}$AYBE SOME people are born with a gardening style they will keep for the rest of their life, but my idea of a good garden has evolved, slowly at first, then with some momentum, now easing up again and refining itself into a style I feel confident and comfortable with. My background, various gardens and garden fashions have all had their part to play, but my first influence, inevitably, was the garden I grew up in. For by all accounts I was virtually born a gardener and there has never been a time when I was not interested in growing plants and in the natural world around me.

ANNE SWITHINBANK

A much loved broadcaster both on television and radio, with an appealing down-to-earth approach to gardening, Anne Swithinbank trained at Kew. She has specialist knowledge of tender plants and is the author of several books on houseplants and gardening under glass, including The Conservatory Gardener, The Gardeners' World Book of House Plants *and* Container Gardening. *Her garden in Devon is a plantsman's paradise and a haven for wildlife, teddy bears and family life.* ❧

    Our family garden was small, but good gardening practices were always in place. Belvedere, just inside Kent, is now part of London's urban sprawl, but when my parents and certainly my grandparents were young, the area was still rural and most people kept chickens, grew vegetables and cultivated rich compost heaps. My father used to rent an allotment, then until recently turned the bottom of a neighbour's plot into a large kitchen garden. I have grown up knowing that everything comes from the soil and, by rights, should end up there as well. I was born in the late fifties, a decade when recycling was a way of life learned during the war. I still have problems throwing away even short lengths of string, have an inclination to drawn nails and store them in tobacco tins and flatten paper bags for re-use. I used to enjoy things like cutting long grass from the driveway, then drying it as hay for our rabbits.

    Quite why I started to grow potted plants in my bedroom, I cannot remember, but by the time I was about eleven, it was jungle-like and virtually impenetrable. The mix of plants was eclectic and dictated largely by what other folk were turning out. No compost heap was left unpilfered. I can remember an arum lily which refused to flower until it was placed outdoors and a large *Fatsia japonica* rescued from the headmistress of the school where my mother was a nursery nurse. *Schefflera elegantissima*, mother-in-law's tongue, mind-your-own-business, busy Lizzies, zebra plant and lemon-scented pelargoniums were typical of the plants around at the time.

We usually enter Kew via the quiet Lion Gate...

Eventually I was presented with half of a small greenhouse (tomatoes and cucumbers occupied the other half) which I filled with cacti, succulents and bedding plants. These I sowed from seed every spring, painstakingly pricking out trayfuls to the illicit blarings of pirate Radio Caroline. Then these carefully nurtured plants would be bedded out in that timeless arrangement of alternating alyssum and lobelia backed up by salvias and marigolds. Mum was my accomplice in this and we soon started experimenting with mimulus, nemesia, fluffy blue-flowered ageratums and daisy-flowered, succulent Livingstone daisies (mesembryanthemums). I was hot on Latin names and, encouraged by Mum, would roll them off, precociously, to astound the aunts and uncles.

So the garden at Belvedere was my first inspiration, which lasted, really, until I turned nineteen and left home with my few possessions, a lot of plants and my budgerigar, Micky, to go and study at Kew. The effect of my three years at the Royal Botanic Gardens must have sunk deep into my psyche and stuck there, only to emerge fairy recently. It is, without doubt, the garden which has influenced me the most and the garden to which I have returned with the most frequency across the years. What I like about Kew is the contrast between areas of concentrated botany and horticulture (as in the glasshouses, rock garden and Duke's Garden) and breathing spaces – the wide-open, park-like expanses of grass and trees. When I look at my newly acquired garden in Devon, I realize I want the same effect on a much smaller scale.

We usually enter Kew via the quiet Lion Gate at the Richmond end of Kew Road. At first, this choice was probably motivated by ease of parking, but the Lion Gate brings visitors into a tranquil end of the gardens, with the best contrast between the busy Kew Road and peaceful open spaces. My children, regular visitors themselves since babyhood, revel in the familiarity of Kew and make a beeline for the drinking fountain hidden in the shrubbery at the side of the path. They may not realize it yet, but they owe their lives to these gardens, which brought their parents together on the same course. I left Kew with a husband as well as a diploma.

Kew's trees are beautiful and historic. To the gardeners of Kew they are as familiar as people and many of them have detailed life histories from the collection of their seed onwards. Their care is taken seriously and during a recent visit, I noticed that wide areas under the canopies of venerable trees in the busiest parts of the garden had been stripped of grass and mulched over with compost to condition the soil, conserve moisture and prevent the trampling of many feet over the fine feeding roots near the soil surface. Some trees are incredibly elderly, making one wonder what the gardens were like when they were planted in the eighteenth century.

On most of our Kew visits, we meander towards the Temperate House. During the period of my training (1976–9) this beautiful old greenhouse was under renovation and at one point my task was to dig over the soil beds inside. Every so often I would drive my dumper truck to the stable yard, load up with well-rotted compost mixed with manure and head back. The entrance to the Temperate House was slippery with mud and as anyone who has driven a dumper will know, they are not the easiest of beasts to steer even under dry conditions. Every time I revved up, aimed for the ramp and through the newly renovated doors, I was relieved not to take them with me. Now the beds are filled with a collection of plants which, typically for Kew, are chosen for their botanical importance over instant impact. The display here is understated, but there are always fascinating plants to see. In winter there are the orange flower trusses of tender New Guinean Vireya rhododendrons and in summer the huge surreal blooms of South African king proteas.

On our more adventurous days, we sometimes take a trip down to Queen Charlotte's Cottage, named for the consort of George III who is thought to have had the house built shortly after the death of his father in 1760. The role of this strange, rather spooky, thatched house would have been as a summer tea room. On the way are areas of long grass which, like other unmown areas at Kew, are maintained for the conservation of butterflies and other insects. A survey conducted in 1992 by the Butterfly Conservation Society noted twenty-three species in the gardens. Apparently a biennial cut allows the eggs and pupae of grassland species to overwinter in long grass. An annual cut during autumn allows plants to seed, areas cut three times in one year encourage nectar-rich flowers and grass maintained at four inches high encourages low-growing wildflowers. My own experiments with meadow management are in their early stages. Allowing grass to grow is the easy part. Weeding out

undesirable docks and ragwort and cutting half an acre of long, thick grass at the end of July is another. Our garden is too small for agricultural machinery, yet hand scything seems a Herculean task, so we experiment with mechanized scythes, small flails and even strimmers.

But now, as visitors, we usually carry on from the Temperate House to the newish Evolution House, for the children to look at the 'bubbling mud' effects. We preferred it in its previous role as the Australian House, full of wattles, correas and banksias. Then on to King William's Temple, where in summer there is much to admire amongst the Mediterranean-style planting on its southern slopes, including rosemaries, rock roses, the dwarf fan palm (*Chamaerops humilis* var. *arborescens*), cotton lavenders, yuccas and a fine Californian headache tree (*Umbellularia californica*). The first time I met one of these I assumed it had earned its common name by curing headaches and crushed a leaf to inhale its fragrance. A few seconds later I was struck by a blinding pain and learnt the hard way that it is a giver of headaches.

Overhead, planes seem to be climbing out of Heathrow at 45-second intervals, taking travellers to all the corners of the globe. It's weird to think that under the roar of their straining engines are plants from every conceivable destination, concentrated into this historic 300-acre garden. Under the bellies of the jets, we usually whisk through the heat of the palm house, looking upward so as not to miss any Dutchman's pipes (*Aristolochia* species) in bloom. Sometimes we bore the children with stories of how Mummy and Daddy used to stamp on cockroaches together as darkness fell during winter. How romantic! The children are usually suffering from horticultural overload by now and want to reach the Princess of Wales Conservatory to see magnificent tropical freshwater fish. My daughter's ambition is to sit on one of the tray-like pads of the giant *Victoria amazonica* waterlily.

After we left Kew, it was ten years before we had the chance to work on a substantial garden of our own and even that measured only one third of an acre. In between, one of my jobs was at Wisley Gardens, where as Glasshouse Supervisor I had the opportunity to indulge my own gardening preferences instead of simply following orders. After five years I had those glasshouses just as I liked them. They were wild, with exotic climbing plants allowed so much headroom they often burgeoned out of the roof vents during summer. Skeins of growth dangled over pathways and visitors used to tangle themselves up in the cat's claw vine (*Macfadyena unguis-cati*) just trying to push their way inside the door. Having seen the exuberance tropical and temperate plants were capable of at Kew and during a visit to the West Indies, I wanted them to have their heads. This was far removed from my humble beginnings in the controlled world of suburban bedding out and I was enjoying myself. Almost every day, one spectacular climber or large shrub after another repaid my efforts by flowering.

> ...out and away through the complicated patterns of glazing bars...

One morning it might be the huge white blooms of herald's trumpet (*Beaumontia grandiflora*) with a natural distribution from India to Vietnam. Then it would be the turn of the fascinating snail flower (*Vigna caracalla*) from tropical America, whose flowers look like clusters of pink snails. A visitor told me it was once a common sight in Australia where this plant was a popular choice for screening outdoor lavatories. The long racemes of the jade vine (*Strongylodon macrobotrys*) and fat strawberries-and-cream buds of *Tecomanthe dendrophila* from New Guinea held me in thrall. I have adored profusion indoors and out ever since and have always felt sorry for those gardeners who feel threatened by growth.

If I learnt to appreciate botany and wild open spaces at Kew and exuberant growth in my Wisley glasshouses, my next lesson was in proportions and it came on a visit to that wonderful garden York Gate at Adel not far outside Leeds. The acre garden is full of detail, yet so well conceived and lovingly constructed, with such an eye for composition, that the wonderful exactness of it all made me want to cry. Oh, how I envy those who visited when the Spencer family were still there.

My most recent inspiration came while working on the French Caribbean Island of Martinique where I fell in love with the gardens surrounding old plantation houses and, in particular, that of Morne Etoile. Water, which collects in a *digue* or reservoir above the estate, flows down through various channels, filling a crayfish pond, and would have tumbled down, finally, to power the now redundant rum distillery at the bottom of the hill. The gardens

themselves are shabbily formal with surprisingly few plants. Huge old lychee trees shadow a lawn, banks of white-flowered *Begonia nitida* shoulder-up against retaining walls and an avenue of tree ferns leads to the back entrance of the main house. All this green and white with old stone and flowing water is unbelievably tranquil, though the odd burst of colour pops up by accident from various garden escapes like hot water plants (achimenes) which have rooted themselves into the walls. Miraculously, Morne Etoile has survived two volcanic eruptions from Mont Pelée, in whose shadow it lies. One was particularly bad and resulted, to the other side of the volcano, in many deaths. Numerous hurricanes have also been withstood and one could easily believe the place is blessed in some way.

I returned from that Caribbean trip to our home in Cobham, where we had spent the last ten years creating our garden on a thin, dry, sandy soil. It is rare for me to leave home for more than a few days at a time and after five weeks' absence I looked at the place with fresh eyes and agreed with John that it was time to move on. During our ten years' stay, the weather had been predominantly hot and dry with several years of drought and I had learnt the wisdom of choosing plants to suit their environment. Although this sounds like common sense, it is surprising how many gardeners struggle to grow totally unsuitable plants and are then puzzled when they die. The trees we used included birches, Judas tree (*Cercis siliquastrum*), Spanish broom (*Spartium junceum*) and large shrubs such as *Clerodendrum trichotomum*. Prairie-style plantings but on a much smaller scale included grasses, hybrid thrifts, honesty, sedums, echinacea and bearded iris. A Mediterranean-style shingle bed dominated by Italian cypress and variegated *Yucca* 'Golden Sword' was a great solution to the dry, impoverished, sun-baked site. Without realizing it, we were in the forefront of fashion with our drifts of low-maintenance, drought-tolerant perennials. John and I had huge fun making that garden, but far from working in harmony, we found we had totally different approaches. We fought, made up, carved up the beds into his and hers, then carried on planting blithely until the garden reached a satisfactory point and we were ready to let it go.

Our current garden, covering a little over an acre and a half, sits right in the rolling Devonshire landscape on the edge of a small town with fields

...sits right in the rolling Devonshire landscape...

on three sides. Gardening so close to the countryside feels like coming home. We have beautiful, very natural hedges of field maple, hawthorn, blackthorn and hazel, woven through with fragrant woodbine and wild roses. A stretch of hazel has recently been laid in traditional Devon/Dorset style and at its foot grows a natural variety of hardy fern which would put many a contrived fernery to shame. The edges of the garden are left wild for birds, butterflies, small mammals and slow worms to breed.

There is enough flat ground around the house for us to have a kitchen garden and play at cultivating as many curious plants as we like, but I would not dream of filling the gentle meadow-like slope with busy plantings. This is our Kew-style breathing space, populated only by a sprinkling of specimen trees and a small orchard, organized into a three-row grid. The rest we allow to grow as meadow threaded through with tightly mown pathways so that we can walk among the wild flowers and meadow brown butterflies. In time, we might add a hazel tunnel to the left-hand margin, with perhaps a bamboo grove and some cool white hydrangeas where the soil is moist and shade dappled.

From my post at the word processor, I constantly turn my head to look through the office door, my gaze passing over a barrage of houseplants on the way. There is the *Begonia rex* I have owned for fourteen years, an unusual, apricot-flowered clivia, a resting azalea, a coffee plant, an *Eucodonia andriexii* 'Naomi' and an unusual, white-flowered, tender *Clerodendrum wallichii*. I smile at the antics of 'my' flock of greenfinches gorging themselves on black sunflower seeds from the bird feeder which hangs from the lower branches of a Japanese cherry. These lower limbs are also home to two hanging baskets. In one lives the hardy squirrel's foot fern, *Davallia mariesii*, and in the other is a staghorn fern, *Platycerium bifurcatum*, which enjoys summers outdoors.

In the middle distance is a foam of cut, blond grasses, waiting to be picked up and composted. They stand out well against the stems of ornamental trees and the hedge abutting my neighbour's garden. The land then falls away to the river valley, originally carved out by a glacier, and swings up the other side to a patchwork of fields and hedges, plummets and rises again to the distance. This view from my office encapsulates my gardening style, itself shaped and influenced by gardens I have known and admired. If you look very closely, you might even find a small patch of bedding plants.

...cultivating as many curious plants as we like...

The Temperate House at Kew was designed by Decimus Burton in 1860
for plants which like a minimum winter temperature of 7°C/45°F.
Taking part in its restoration, completed in 1982, was an honour,
even if my role was only to dig the soil beds inside.

My favourite view (below) is from the balcony, accessed by spiral wrought-iron staircases. Look down on the tops of tree ferns (Dicksonia antartica) or out and away through the complicated pattern of glazing bars, beyond this concentration of greenery, to acres of plants and trees.

The giant Amazon waterlily (Victoria amazonica) flourishes inside the carefully controlled, humid environment of the Princess of Wales Conservatory (overleaf). Special viewing windows in the sides of the tank reveal the strong, prickly veins which, full of spongy tissue, give the huge leaves their buoyancy.

The Palm House is home to some amazing tropical climbers, so it pays to look up at regular intervals. The South American birthworts (Aristolochias) bear strange, mottled flowers, some tailed, some huge like ungainly bats. Their foul smell attracts insects, which become imprisoned to effect pollination.

In one corner of Kew is a handful of venerable specimens, propped and cabled like old men leaning on sticks. This locust tree (Robinia pseudoacacia) is a relic from the original botanic gardens, founded in 1759 by Princess Augusta, mother of George III.

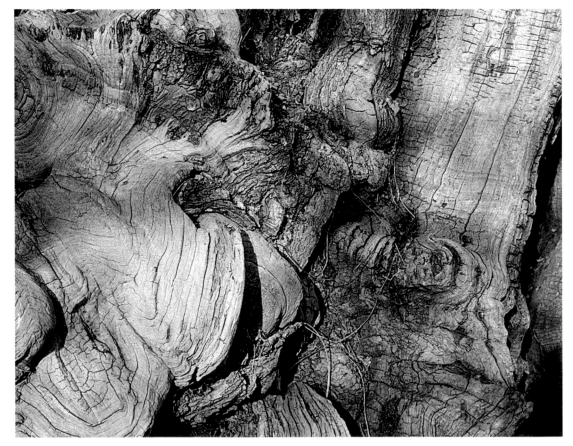

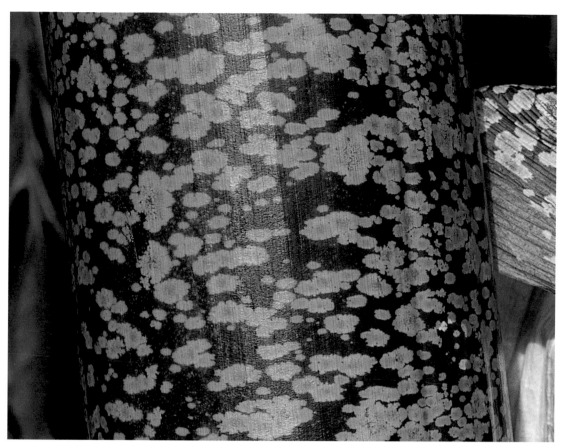

The Sumatran titan arum (Amorphophallus titanum) *is one Kew's triumphs, attracting much press coverage and, in the process, huge crowds when it bloomed in the Princess of Wales Conservatory for the first time in 1996. Rising up on a stout, mottled stalk, the inflorescence often reaches a height of six feet.*

Large, mulched circles beneath mature trees protect their roots from trampling in much-visited areas of the garden. This brings its own rewards when the dark fibrous mulch acts as a backdrop to the freshly fallen leaves of a majestic London plane (Platanus orientalis), *planted in 1762.*

As Far as the Eye Can See

by ROSEMARY VEREY

The wall surrounding the garden at Barnsley House shuts out the countryside beyond. Rather than creating views that stretch as far as the eye can see, as David Hicks did at The Grove, we have made vistas within our walls. Simon Verity's stone gardener, standing by the climber-clad wall (left), seems to be turning to visitors, as if to invite them to explore.

Walking in a garden, when the owners

have asked me to help them, thoughts for vistas, paths and borders flash through my mind. These are ideas carried in my memory from gardens I know or individual features I have seen on my travels. There are thoughts for colour, sometimes unexpected, such as the artist Bob Dash uses to paint fences and gates at Sagaponack in Long Island. Bob's garden is designed with bravado, with mirrors and a grove of *Ginkgo biloba*, created by planting young trees close together so their branches become entwined. Through Bob's influence, I painted one of our garden doors,

ROSEMARY VEREY OBE

An internationally renowned plantswoman and garden designer, Rosemary Verey – who died in May 2001 – worked in her garden at Barnsley House in Gloucestershire come rain or shine. Her clients included HRH The Prince of Wales and Elton John. She was one of the most highly regarded and engaging of garden writers and the author of a host of gardening classics, including The Garden in Winter *and* Good Planting. The Making of a Garden *is an in-depth account of Barnsley, the garden that attracts thousands of visitors from all over the world and which is frequently featured on television. She held the RHS Victoria Medal of Honour and received the Garden Writers' Guild Lifetime Achievement Award.* ✤

set in a mellow Cotswold stone wall, a cardinal red. Having fun with colour reminds me of Christopher Lloyd's ever-vital planting ideas. When I walk along the path where we have planted shell-pink *Oenothera speciosa* with orange eschscholzias, I think of his garden at Great Dixter in Sussex.

The sun's rays have a subtle effect on colour, a point I noted in the 1980s, after visiting Peggy Rockefeller's garden in Seal Harbor, Maine. Originally designed for her in-laws by Beatrix Farrand, the two main borders in the heart of Peggy's garden were planted for spectacular summer displays: hot colours – red, orange, yellow and purple – to show at their best in evening sunlight; cool pastel shades – pink, blue, lilac, white and grey – in the east-facing border where the morning sun would give depth. I tucked these thoughts away in my mind twenty years ago and they are useful.

I think of Russell Page who had a great influence on my approach to garden design, particularly with regard to water and the placing of trees. His intimate garden at the Frick Museum, in the heart of New York City, has a stretch of water that reflects the building and the planting – all is cool and green in contrast to the street outside. A frequent visitor to Barnsley House, Russell said that water should add sound, give movement and create reflections; and, if you fill a pool with plants hiding the water's surface, you might as well have a lawn. Think of the waterlilies at Giverny, how Monet had the leaves cut back every day so they formed floating rafts. Keep the planting restrained and

allow space for reflections of the sky and clouds, as well as surrounding trees and shrubs. Our octagonal pool reflects the temple and, for movement and sound, we have a fountain at the end of the temple vista. Water spouting from four stone frogs catches the light and makes gentle splashing music.

I remember a day spent at the Pepsico headquarters at Purchase, New York, when Russell was laying out a bare bank near the building. He had a mass of plants which he was carefully placing in position. He would stand back to see the effect, making sure the spacing was correct, and walk round to see how they would look from every angle. Russell loved trees, especially moisture-loving willows, alders and swamp cypress. It was through his influence that we planted willows here at Barnsley, to enjoy the early catkins, and I accepted the fact that on dry ground they would perform less well than beside a stream.

I think of Bill and Nancy Frederick's American stroll garden in Delaware, created over many years but forever evolving. I visit there often and on every occasion I am reminded of the importance of planting in bold, broad strokes, where there is space. For example, Bill uses a single species, *Berberis thunbergii* 'Atropurpurea Nana' (syn. *B.t.* 'Crimson Pygmy'), along a path as it ascends the hill and forsythia in the distance to echo his golden dogwood. His wisterias are memorable, too – trained as single-trunk, twelve-foot trees, supported by stout galvanized pipes. Nancy grows vegetables in raised beds, filled with imported topsoil. She practises strict crop rotation and mulches the beds in the autumn with manure, mushroom compost or leaf mould to keep them thoroughly productive. I have been advising clients who garden on poor or sloping ground to do this ever since I saw how successful it was for Nancy.

These thoughts make me realize how essential it is to travel and see other people's ideas, as well as to be open to the influence of good garden design and practice. But there is a subtle difference between influence and inspiration and a garden nearer home, in Oxfordshire, is one I would single out as a constant source of inspiration. David Hicks who created it had a strong sense of design, discipline and feeling for structure. He had been a successful interior designer for twenty-six years when he and his wife Pamela, daughter of Lord and Lady Mountbatten, moved to The Grove, an eighteenth-century farm-house with acres of land but no garden. What could be more fitting than that he should look out of the windows of the rooms he had just decorated and make the garden a natural extension of these? The three main rooms – the drawing room facing south, the dining room facing west and the library looking to the drive and front gate – all have striking views, some stretching as far as the eye can see, each with its own character. Now when I visit a client I ask to look from the windows of the main rooms, including the kitchen and bedrooms. I take photographs and make sketches – it is easy to think you will remember a pattern, but it is wise to draw it, however roughly. Lanning Roper advised me to make 'tidy and comprehensive notes' after seeing a garden. 'Before you go to bed,' he said, 'and before you forget the detail.' Taking photographs is essential as a reminder of the slope of the terrain, the existing trees, the perspective and distances. In his books, David Hicks shared with us his method of putting tracing paper over a photograph of a scene or patch he wished to improve, then drawing different ideas on to this until he found the best solution.

The Grove has inspired me in many other ways, in particular encouraging me to forget the obvious and not to be dull, for there is often an exciting, unusual answer to a problem. Use striking colours, just as David did in his interiors. (A red cushion will catch the eye but too much red in the garden can be distracting.) Exploit the infinite variety of the colour green – David described his garden as 'an essentially green-on-green space'. Keep in mind the element of surprise, using apertures to create different moods – of excitement as well as calm. Remember, too, to plant for the future generation – David planted thousands of trees, which, he wrote, 'my grandchildren will enjoy'. And now let me take you to The Grove so I can explain how David's vision has stretched beyond his lifetime.

Over the years since David started creating the garden, the vista from the drawing room has developed and now reaches dramatically into the distance. Clearly he had absorbed and admired the work of Le Nôtre in France, how the *allées* and avenues create the feeling that the property stretches as far as the eye can see. (No problem in Louis XIV's time.) David advocated well-defined structure, a formal and tidy look near the house. Box-edged beds were filled with lavender, santolina and forget-me-nots with spring bulbs, followed by

...David described his garden as 'an essentially green-on-green space'.

...enjoy their June moment of colour.

summer bedding. But even this simple planting was soon replaced by more box, to give the effect of green steps. An elegant statue of Flora overlooks the parterre but to prevent her dominating and seeming too grand, her plinth is low. There is a rise in the lawn towards a green theme, where stretches of longer grass on each side are backed by lines of hornbeams on eight-foot trunks, underplanted with a clipped hornbeam hedge. These are well tailored and kept to the correct dimensions. There is a gated clairvoyée, beyond this a green 'tent' of clipped hornbeam and further beyond a long avenue of Spanish chestnuts.

On the west side of the house, looking from the dining room, the perfectly symmetrical view has as much appeal on a misty day as it does in summer sunshine. Most of us have the idea that a swimming pool is an eyesore and we must hide it behind a solid hedge or a wall so the bathers will not be over-looked. The Hicks' pool, in full view of the window, is designed to look like a canal, the sides and base painted black, and the surround is constructed using different textures. First, there is a foot-wide stone edging, then a slightly wider band of cobblestones set in cement, then comes the green grass, a soothing and unifying element. This simply designed space has standard horse chest-nuts planted in two 'L' shapes on each side.

A further key to the success of the scene is another wide avenue of Spanish chestnuts stretching for a quarter of a mile into the distance and ending with a narrow opening cut through a belt of trees to suggest a vista of enormous distance. Wildlife plays a part, with flocks of rooks flying over in the evening, the occasional deer grazing, and once when I was there a buzzard came into sight, looking for prey. To me, it is a lesson that we must always be aware of the beauty of the countryside which envelops our garden, whether we are the owner of the acres or can 'borrow the view'.

Two more points I learnt from this swimming pool area: how important it is to keep all branches of climbers trained firmly against the house, never allowing them to obscure the view from inside or spoil the symmetry on the outside; and when choosing climbers and other shrubs to be planted close to the house, think of the colour of the façade as well as your clients' whims.

When David and Pammy entertained he loved to make large flower arrangements for the drawing room. Hidden away behind a wall, in a far corner, is the cutting garden. David called this the Secret Garden and it is the only place where he allowed mixtures of bright colours, describing the effect as 'poppies, tree peonies, roses, lilies and foxgloves jostling each other for one's attention'. Scent fills the air but we must not loiter, there is so much more to see. When David was alive, if the drawbridge was up, it was a sign that he was busy, so visitors could not cross the shallow moat to the pavilion, given to him by Pammy for his sixtieth birthday. This building, designed by David, with ogee gothick windows and a crenellated roof, is the focus of an area of smaller spaces.

We make our way to the green Pot Garden. First, near the pavilion, we come to two rectangular blocks of hawthorn (clipped to sixteen inches), with pots of artichokes dropped into them, typical of David's interpretation of green on green and his ingenious use of plants. The containers in the Pot Garden stand on squares of gravel and all are painted green, most of them bottomless so the plants – architectural box, *Sedum* 'Herbstfreude' (Autumn Joy) and *Crambe cordifolia* – can root through into the soil. Ever practical, David did this to cut down on watering and maintenance: the containers are lifted off and stored in a barn for the winter.

This green garden leads into the Red Room, very small and intimate, with 'walls' of copper beach and a narrow opening framing the focal point, an urn with the calming sound of water tumbling down its mossy sides. David disliked copper beeches in the landscape, their colour, he felt, looking 'out of place among the soft greens of England'. Here, the hedge's deep red leaves are brightened by *Rosa* 'Danse du Feu' climbing through it and the gravel floor sparkles with fallen rose petals.

From here we can wander along the tunnel through the centre of the old walled garden, planted with climbing 'American Pillar' roses, short-blooming so enjoy their June moment of colour. Also for June, David planted flax in the distance to create a powder-blue haze through his landscape. I was at The Grove the day a clearing was being cut through a tree plantation to create yet another vista into the distance. Some time later an ugly bungalow was built (not on Hicks land). This had to be hidden, so resourceful David positioned the old trailer-based pyramid in his field to conceal it.

This brings us to the view from the library window of a large ilex surrounded by rough grass and, beyond, a ha-ha and clumps of trees. This view, which David described as 'less contrived' than the ones from the drawing and dining rooms, is also the view from the front door, so visitors leave with a lasting feeling of satisfaction. From here and from his study window, David could see if the front gate was shut – essential to keep out the deer. He cut a hole in a large holly tree to do this. David always had an answer and this is why he was such a good friend and would help me with problems.

David wrote: 'I would rather have monumental acres than small areas minutely manicured.' He had the acres and designed them with a feeling of space and openness, declaring that he would never have herbaceous borders, nor flowers that could be seen from the house. At Barnsley, we have the small areas and enjoy exuberant plantings, always aiming to improve the borders. So it may seem contradictory that David's clearly defined theories have been a strong influence on me, and The Grove is a constant source of inspiration. But, like David, I believe a firm structure is the basis of a successful garden and our own solution has been to make vistas within the walls surrounding our garden. The broad sweeping view across the garden in winter changes in spring as the shrubs burst into leaf and again in summer when the perennials stand tall. I like to plant in layers, with early bulbs, narcissus and tulips coming through forget-me-nots, and herbaceous and flowering shrubs following to create colour and interest in every season. I advocate planting to entice you out of the house during the coldest months, using coloured stems, scented winter shrubs and the earliest flowering bulbs. Views from various resting places give us time to pause, look and see. Even our potager has vistas to discover as you walk among the vegetables.

Of course, everything at Barnsley is on a much smaller scale than at The Grove, but analyzing why the shapes, spaces and structures succeed in David's garden has helped me to see as well as to look. Walking round our garden, I think of the people who have influenced me and the gardens I find inspiring, but when I arrive home after a visit to The Grove, I see things with fresh and critical eyes.

> Views from various resting places give us time to pause, look and see. Even our potager has vistas to discover as you walk among the vegetables.

David Hicks, always full of original ideas, created new designs for his garden gates at The Grove. Solid at the base, the top allows you to see through, inviting you into the next garden. Here, the pleached hornbeams beyond are precisely clipped.

A more complex gate pattern (above), but you are encouraged to walk through and along the mown path. Pause awhile on the bench, sheltered by the old farm building. Scented plants or clipped box in terracotta containers lead the way and fragrant climbers waft on the air.

The narrow opening in the beech hedge (right) gives a view into the farmland. The mown path is kept narrow by the neatly trimmed hedge. With her camera, Vivian Russell has caught David's hunters enjoying their summer grazing.

Standard horse chestnuts flank David's swimming pool (preceding pages), designed to look like a canal.

The strong, formal line of a hornbeam avenue (right), underplanted with grasses mown twice a year, leads to the rustic arbour with its stumpwork and natural architecture.

David's natural flair for vistas with a transition from light to shade gives this view (left, below) added excitement, especially in summer when the plants soften the severe lines of the mown grass path.

Before you leave The Grove, have another look at the formal garden beside the house (below). Here sixteen rectangular box-edged beds are presided over by the statue of Flora which the Hicks brought from their previous garden at Britewell. David's garden design work was based on his experience of gardening in Oxfordshire, as well as on his knowledge of gardens in Europe, South Africa and the United States of America.

Gardens to Visit

Barnsley House

Cranborne Manor

The gardens mentioned in the text and listed here may be visited by the general public; some are open on a regular basis; others only on specific days.

Gardens prefixed with the letters:

APP may be visited by appointment only. Please telephone to check on opening dates and times.

NT belong to the National Trust or equivalent organizations outside the UK
www.nationaltrust.org.uk

EH indicate gardens managed by English Heritage
www.english-heritage.org.uk

NGS indicates gardens in England and Wales open through the National Gardens Scheme
Tel +44 (0) 1483 211537
email ngs@ngs.co.uk
www.ngs.org.uk

The Garden Conservancy in the United States of America opens 400 gardens in 23 states
Tel +1 914 265 2029
email gardencons@aol.com
www.gardenconservancy.org

ENGLAND

NGS BARNSLEY HOUSE
(Mr & Mrs Charles Verey)
Barnsley, Near Cirencester, Gloucestershire
Tel +44 (0) 1285 740561
Open Mondays, Wednesdays, Thursdays and Saturdays, February to Christmas

EH BELSAY HALL
Newcastle-upon-Tyne
Tel +44 (0) 1661 881636
Open daily except 1 January and 24 to 26 December

NGS THE BETH CHATTO GARDENS
Elmstead Market, Essex
Tel +44 (0) 1206 822007
Open Monday to Saturday, March to October; Monday to Friday, November to February; closed on Bank Holidays

NGS CRANBORNE MANOR
(The Viscount & Viscountess Cranborne)
Cranborne, Dorset
Tel +44 (0) 1725 517248
Open Wednesdays, March to September

NGS DENMANS
(John Brookes)
Fontwell, Sussex
Tel +44 (0) 1243 542 808
Open daily, March to October, or by appointment

NGS East Lambrook Manor Garden
(Robert & Marianne Williams)
East Lambrook, South Petherton, Somerset
Tel +44 (0) 1460 240328
Open 10am to 5pm, Monday to Saturday, all year

NGS FOLLY FARM
(Sir Desmond & Lady Pitcher)
Sulhamstead, Berkshire

NGS GREAT DIXTER
(Christopher Lloyd)
Northiam, East Sussex
Tel +44 (0) 1797 253107
Open 2 to 5pm, Tuesday to Sunday, April to October

HAMPTON COURT PALACE
East Molesey, Surrey
Tel +44 (0) 20 8781 9500
King's privy garden open daily, all year

Great Dixter

Hestercombe Gardens

Levens Hall

ngs Hestercombe Gardens
(Mr P. White)
Cheddon Fitzpaine, Somerset
Tel +44 (0) 1823 413923
Open daily, all year

nt/ngs Hidcote Manor Garden
Chipping Camden, Gloucestershire
Tel +44 (0) 1386 438333
Open daily except Tuesday and
Friday, 1 April to 5 November

ngs Levens Hall
(C.H. Bagot Esq)
Kendal, Cumbria
Tel +44 (0) 15395 60321
Open Sunday to Thursday,
1 April to 14 October

ngs Mapperton Gardens
(The Earl & Countess of Sandwich)
Near Beaminster, Dorset
Tel +44 (0) 1308 862645

ngs The Old Rectory
(Charles & Mary Keen)
Duntisbourne Rous, Gloucestershire

ngs The Old Vicarage
(Alan Gray & Graham Robeson)
East Ruston, Norfolk

ngs Renishaw Hall
(Sir Reresby & Lady Sitwell)
Renishaw, Derbyshire
Tel +44 (0) 1777 860755

Royal Botanic Gardens, Kew
Richmond, Surrey
Tel +44 (0) 20 8940 1171
Open daily except Christmas and
New Year's Day

ngs Royal Horticultural
Society Garden at Wisley
Wisley, Surrey
Tel +44 (0) 1483 224234
Open daily except Christmas Day
(Sundays, March to October, RHS
members and their guests only)

ngs Saling Hall
(Mr & Mrs Hugh Johnson)
Great Saling, Essex

nt/ngs Sissinghurst Castle
Garden
Sissinghurst, near Cranbrook, Kent
Tel +44 (0) 1580 710700
Open Tuesday to Sunday,
April 1 to October 15

nt/ngs Stowe Landscape Gardens
Buckingham, Buckinghamshire
Tel +44 (0) 1280 822437
Open Wednesday to Sunday, 29
March to 29 October

nt Studley Royal
Fountains, Ripon, North Yorkshire
Tel +44 (0) 1765 608888
Open daily, all year, except Fridays,
from November to January, and
24 to 25 December

ngs Sutton Place
(Sutton Place Foundation)
Guildford, Surrey
Tel +44 (0) 1483 504455

nt/ngs Tintinhull
Farm Street, Tintinhull, Somerset
Tel +44 (0) 1935 822545
Open Wednesday to Sunday,
April to September

ngs York Gate
Back Church Lane, Adel, Leeds,
Yorkshire
Tel +44 (0) 113 2678240

France

app La Bonne Maison
(Odile Masquelier's rose garden)
99 chemin de Fontanières,
69350 La Mulatière/Lyon
Tel +33 (0) 478 42 42 82
Open March and April: Monday,
Friday, Saturday; 1 May to 15 June:
Monday to Saturday. From 9am to
1pm

GIVERNY

NINFA

VILLA D'ESTE

app LES COLOMBIÈRES
Menton, Riviera
Tel +33 (0) 492 1097 10
(Maison de Patrimoine)

app CRECH AR PAPE
22820 Plougrescant, Brittany
Tel +33 (0) 296 92 55 89

GIVERNY
Fondation Claude Monet, Giverny
Tel +33 (0) 232 51 28 21
Open April to October,
daily except Mondays

GERMANY

WESTPARK
(public garden)
Munich
Open daily

ITALY

BOMARZO
Sacro Bosso/Villa Orsini, Parco dei
Mostri, Viterbo, Lazio
Tel +39 0761 92 40 29
Open daily

CASTELLO DI CELSA
Località Rosia, Sovicille (SI)
Tel +39 06 68307326

NINFA
Giardino e Rovine de Ninfa,
Sermoneta (LT)
Tel +39 0773 69 54 04 17
Open April to October, first
Saturday and Sunday of the month

VILLA CAPPONI
Pian dei Giullari, Florence

VILLA CHIGI CETINALE
(Lord Lambton)
Sovicille, 53018 Siena
Tel +39 0577 2209 (tourist office)

VILLA D'ESTE
Piazza Trento 1, 00019 Tivoli
(Roma)
Tel +39 0774 312070

VILLA GAMBERAIA
Via del Rosselino 72, 50135 Firenze-
Settignano
Tel +39 055 697205

VILLA LANTE
Via J. Barozzi 71, 01031 Bagnaia
(VT), Viterbo
Tel +39 0761 288088

VILLA LA FOCE
63 Strada della Vittoria, 53042
Chianciano Terme, Siena
Tel +39 0578 69101

VILLA MEDICI
Viale Trinità dei Monti 1, Fiesole,
Roma
Tel +39 06 679 83 81
Open March to June and 6 to 25
October

VILLA REALE
Via Fraga Alta, Marlia
Tel +39 0583 30108

VILLA VICOBELLO
Via Vicobello 12, Vico Alto Siena
Tel +39 0577 2209

JAPAN

app RYOAN-JI
Ukkyo-ku, Kyoto
Tel +81 (0) 75 463-2216

NETHERLANDS

PIET OUDOLF'S GARDEN
Broekstraat 17, 6999 DE Hummelo
Tel +31 (0) 4 381120
Open in June and August
(nursery open March to November)

Levi's Plaza

Madoo

Portmeirion

Scotland

app Charles Jencks'
cosmological garden
Tel +44 (0) 1387 263066
Open one day per year

Little Sparta
(Ian Hamilton Finlay)
Dunsyre, near Lanark, Lanarkshire
Open mid-June to September,
Friday and Sunday, 2pm to 5pm
Tel +44 (0) 1555 661661
(Lanark tourist office)

United States of America

Bloedel Reserve
7571 NE Dolphin Drive, Bainbridge
Island, Washington DC
Open Wednesday to Sunday
except federal holidays
Tel +1 206 842-7631

Fallingwater
Route 381, Mill Run, Pennsylvania
Tel +1 724-329-8501
Open Tuesday to Friday

nt Filoli
Canada Road, San Francisco,
California
Open Tuesday to Saturday
Tel +1 415 364-2880

Frick Museum
1 E 70th St (5th Avenue),
New York City
Tel +1 212 288 0700
Open daily except Mondays

Huntingdon Botanic Garden
1151 Oxford Rd, Los Angeles,
California
Tel +1 818 405-2100
Open daily except Mondays

Ira's Fountain
SW 3rd & Clay, Portland, Oregon
Open daily

Levi's Plaza
(public garden)
San Francisco
Open daily

Madoo
(Bob Dash)
Sagaponack, Long Island, New York
Tel +1 516 537 8200
Open May to September,
Monday and Wednesday

app El Novillero
Dewey Donnell Garden, Sonoma,
Sonoma County, California
Tel +1 707 996 1090 (tourist office)

Seattle Freeway Park
Seattle, Washington DC
Open daily

Taliesin West
108th Street North At Cactus Road,
Scottsdale, Arizona
Tel +1 602860 8810
Open daily 9am to 4pm

app Vineyard Garden
(Molly Chappellet)
1581 Sage Canyon Road
St Helena, California
Tel +1 707 963 7136
email info@chappellet.com

Wales

nt/ngs Powis Castle & Garden
Welshpool, Powys
Tel +44 (0) 1938 554338
Open Wednesday to Sunday
plus Bank Holiday Mondays,
1 April to 29 October

Portmeirion
Gwynedd
Tel +44 (0) 1766 770228
Open daily, all year

Index

Page numbers in *italic* refer to the illustrations